Whale Watch

Vic Cockcroft and Peter Joyce

Struik Publishers (Pty) Ltd
(a member of The Struik New Holland Publishing Group (Pty) Ltd)
Cornelis Struik House
80 McKenzie Street
Cape Town
8001

Reg. No. 54/00965/07

First published 1998

4 6 8 10 9 7 5 3

Designer: Janice Evans
Managing editor: Pippa Parker
Editor: Peter Joyce
Editorial assistant: Giséle Raad
Design assistant: Lellyn Creamer
MTN Whale Route consultant: Darden Lotz
Picture researcher: Carmen Swanepoel
Cartographers: John Loubser and Mark Seabrook

Reproduction by Hirt & Carter, Cape Town
Printed and bound by NBD
Drukkery Street, Goodwood, Western Cape.

FRONT COVER: A humpback whale breaching.
TITLE PAGE: The tail flukes of a southern right whale rise
above the waters of Algoa Bay.
BACK COVER: (in clockwise order): Cape fur seal mother and pup;
a common dolphin; the tail flukes of a humpback whale;
whale-watching at Hermanus.

ISBN: 1 86872 163 9

The publishers and The MTN Whale Route wish to thank:
MTN; the Western Cape Tourism Board; the Garden Route
Regional Tourism Organisation; the Cape Overberg Tourism
Association; the Helderberg Tourism Bureau; Swartland and
Sandveld Tourism, and the West Coast Tourism Organisation.
Our sincere thanks also go to each individual member of these
various tourism bodies for their courteous co-operation in
accumulating and verifying the information. We must also record
our gratitude to two Cape Town-based institutions:
the South African Maritime Museum, V & A Waterfront; and the
Sea Fisheries Research Institute, in particular to Mike Meyer,
Pierre Malan and Tony van Dalsen.

Contents

Sponsor's Foreword

The waters off the coast of southern Africa are visited by more than forty different kinds of marine mammal, among them the southern right whale – arguably the most striking and most frequently seen of the larger cetaceans along the MTN Whale Route.

This extraordinary diversity, together with the superb opportunities the region offers for land-based whale watching, has attracted a great deal of local and international interest to these mysterious marine creatures which, in turn, has created a real need for more information on the various species found in the wider southern African waters, their physical nature and distribution, habits and habitats. *Whale Watch* will help fulfil this need, providing visitors with a coast to coast guide to the subcontinent's best whale, dolphin and seal watching spots – especially those along the 900-kilometre seaboard from Strandfontein in the west to Tsitsikamma in the east (the MTN Whale Route) – together with profiles of each and every marine mammal that might be encountered on a southern African whale-watching expedition.

The MTN Whale Route strives to inform and educate all those who visit the Cape coastline, and we are proud to add *Whale Watch* to our various information tools. We hope and believe it will answer the many questions that people ask about the marine mammals they can see, and about the environments in which they live.

GREG VOGT

CHAIRMAN: MTN WHALE ROUTE
Founded February 1996

Introduction

Southern Africa's seaboard, running more than 4 000 km from northern Namibia around to the mouth of the Zambezi River in Mozambique, provides marvellously revealing windows into the world of whales, dolphins, seals and dugongs.

The region is best known, perhaps, for its southern right whales, large (up to 60-ton), callus-encrusted cetaceans that migrate into the coastal waters to mate and to nurse their calves. They arrive from their chilly Antarctic feeding grounds in the winter and springtime months, making their way close inshore to provide whale-watchers with some of the best land- and boat-based viewing opportunities in the world.

Early open-boat whalers took a devastating toll of right whale numbers – it is reckoned that around 12 000 of them were killed between 1790 and 1825 – and later commercial hunters, using more efficient methods, continued the slaughter, not only of these but of many other species. Then, happily, the authorities stepped in. In 1935 the southern right became the first large whale to receive the protection of the law, and since then strict international control has been extended to the whaling industry as a whole. As a result, this and other cetacean populations have staged a splendid recovery.

Many of the marine mammals featured in these pages are 'inshore' animals, those which occur in the relatively shallow (that is, less than 200 m deep) waters of the region's continental shelf. This, for the most part, is wide – especially so along the west and south coasts, though it narrows significantly in the east. Altogether, 44 species can, at various times and places and at different frequencies, be sighted from vantage points on headland, cliff and beach. In some places – for example at Hermanus, Plettenberg and Algoa bays and, especially, along the Transkei coast – the animals come within a hundred or so metres of the shoreline.

Close-up whale viewing above Walker Bay, near Hermanus on the southern seaboard.

Pride of the region are the southern rights. Other species include the 40-ton humpback whale, which migrates northwards between May and December each year to its breeding grounds off the coasts of Angola and Mozambique; Bryde's whale, occurring all year round but rather further out from the coast; and the minke and pygmy minke, which are deep-water mammals but they do sometimes make their way into the shallower reaches. The killer whale or orca (of 'Free Willy' fame), striking in its black and white markings, can occasionally be seen in all seasons (its appearance is highly unpredictable), most often between Lüderitz and Walvis Bay in Namibia and in the Plettenberg and Algoa bay areas of the southern seaboard.

And then there are the dolphins, among them the bottlenose and humpback (both stay close inshore, in waters no more than 30 m deep), the common, Heaviside's and the occasional spotted species. Cape fur seals are present throughout the region; though they are generally not found en masse on the coast itself – the biggest of the concentrations are to be seen on the various offshore islands and, most notably, in Namibia's Cape Cross reserve north of Swakopmund.

ABOUT THIS BOOK

MTN Whale Watch is divided into three parts. The first, comprising features on the history of whaling and the nature and habits of whales, introduces the subject.

The second part has a somewhat wider application: it is intended for the whale-watcher who is also a tourist – on the assumption that few whale enthusiasts, however dedicated, want to spend every single hour of their visit aboard a boat or gazing out to sea. It covers the main points of general (largely environmental) interest along the coasts as well as the prime whale and

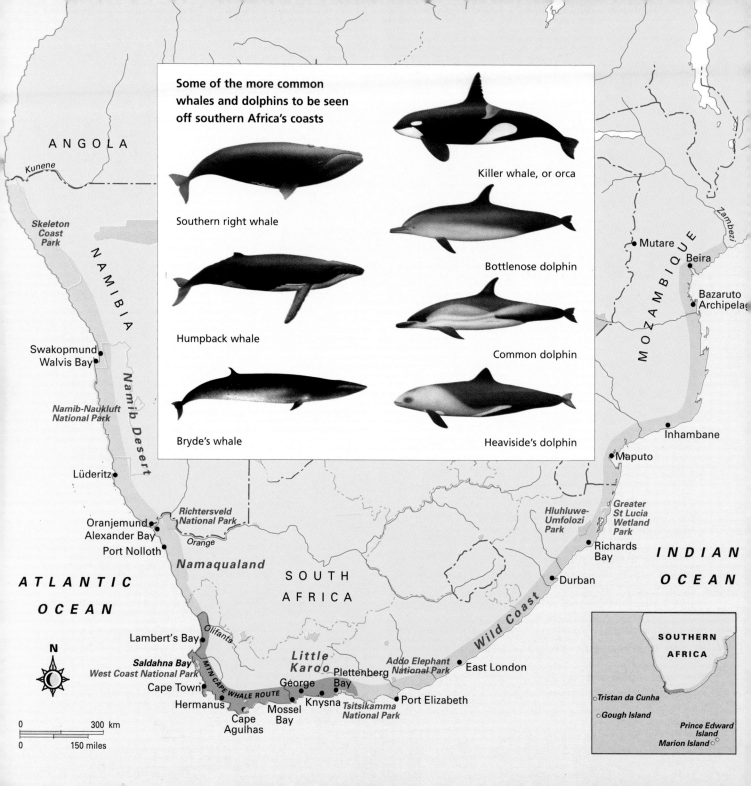

Some of the more common whales and dolphins to be seen off southern Africa's coasts

Southern right whale

Humpback whale

Bryde's whale

Killer whale, or orca

Bottlenose dolphin

Common dolphin

Heaviside's dolphin

ANGOLA

Kunene

NAMIBIA

Skeleton Coast Park

Swakopmund
Walvis Bay

Namib Desert

Namib-Naukluft National Park

Lüderitz

Oranjemund
Alexander Bay
Port Nolloth

Richtersveld National Park

Orange

Namaqualand

SOUTH AFRICA

ATLANTIC OCEAN

Lambert's Bay

Olifants

Saldanha Bay
West Coast National Park

Cape Town

Hermanus

Cape Agulhas

Little Karoo

George

Mossel Bay

Knysna

Plettenberg Bay

Tsitsikamma National Park

Addo Elephant National Park

Port Elizabeth

East London

Wild Coast

Durban

Richards Bay

Hluhluwe-Umfolozi Park

Greater St Lucia Wetland Park

Maputo

Inhambane

MOZAMBIQUE

Zambezi

Mutare

Beira

Bazaruto Archipelago

INDIAN OCEAN

MTN CAPE WHALE ROUTE

N

0   300 km

0   150 miles

SOUTHERN AFRICA

Tristan da Cunha

Gough Island

Prince Edward Island

Marion Island

A southern right whale begins to 'breach', thrusting its massive body above the water to fall back with a mighty splash. The reasons for this behaviour are not entirely clear.

state they can be difficult to spot.

◆ Southern rights remain in or near a particular part of the coast for a number of days so, again, be patient: it's usually worth waiting for good weather conditions before sallying forth on a viewing expedition.

◆ Watch for the whale's spout, or blow – invariably the first sign of its presence (see page 12).

◆ Southern rights can be identified by the callosities on their heads (page 50), and by the absence of a dorsal fin. Non-maternal animals are seen in groups of up to seven; females with calves are usually on their own.

◆ Some do's and don'ts: don't venture onto private property without first seeking permission; treat the land, and especially its plant life, with respect; hold noise and activity levels down (whales are sensitive to disturbance); keep safety well in mind, particularly on cliff-tops and on shore-line rocks; be careful of the sea at all times: waves can be unpredictable.

◆ Make use of MTN's Whale Hotline (see box).

◆ For boat-based viewing, take binoculars, camera, barrier cream, and anti-nausea precautions if you're prone to seasickness. Make sure that the skipper has the required permit, and follow his advice and instructions at all times; don't make unnecessary noise or movement.

dolphin viewing areas. Here, emphasis is placed on one particular stretch of southern Africa's seaboard, the 900 km between Strandfontein in the west and Tsitsikamma in the east. This is the MTN Whale Route, designed by that company to combine the challenges and pleasures of whale-watching with an insight into the scenic, floral, faunal and cultural character of the various areas. Some 100 interpretative signboards, posters filled with useful information, have been erected at prime and easily accessible sites along the way.

The final section of the book is devoted to the marine mammals themselves, in a series of informative species profiles prepared by leading marine scientist Vic Cockcroft.

WHALE-WATCHING TIPS

Only bona fide researchers and licenced commercial whale-watching enterprises are allowed to approach by boat within 300 m of a whale. And certain areas, including Hermanus's Walker Bay, are classed as no-go zones.

◆ For shore-based viewing, you'll need a good pair of binoculars, a camera (200 mm lens), a hat and barrier cream to keep the sun at bay, and plenty of patience.

◆ Clear, wind-free conditions are the best, though they also tend to lull the whales into a kind of sleepy indolence. In this

---

THE MTN WHALE HOTLINE

Land-based whale-viewing, even in the best of seasons, is a bit of a lottery: these marine mammals sometimes turn up in unexpected places, leave favoured areas deserted for days on end and, generally, show very little concern for those waiting and watching on shore. A call to the Hotline will point you in just the right direction, saving you a great deal of time and trouble. The toll-free number is 083 910 1028. Otherwise, phone Cape Town (021) 401 7347, or e-mail cwr_master@mtn.co.za. More general information on the MTN Whale Route is available on Internet site http://www.cape-whaleroute.co.za

Whaling through the Ages

Humankind has hunted and scavenged the whales of the oceans since pre-historic times, when the bones of these great marine mammals were used for, among other things, the rafters of dwellings. Early folk also relished the flesh: whale bones have been found in Neolithic kitchen middens along the coast of Denmark.

The Inuit (Eskimo) people of Greenland, and of arctic Asia and America, actively pursued marine mammals after they perfected a way of retrieving harpoons that missed their mark. These hardy people used single and double cockpit kayaks (light-framed boats covered with animal skins) and harpoons fitted with floats to hunt seals, narwhals and, now and then, bowhead whales.

Early in the 10th century, the Japanese may have practised a type of primitive whaling, using rowing boats to herd long-finned pilot whales into the shallows. Similarly, there are records, preserved in the Faeroe Islands and dating from 1584, which show that catches of up to 1 700 such 'driven' whales were being landed each year.

EARLY WHALING IN SOUTHERN AFRICA

Certain bays along the African coastline are regularly visited each spring by southern right whales, who come close inshore to mate and calve. Humpback whales use the coastline as a migratory route to and from their tropical breeding grounds. The movements of both species have placed them well within view of the shore for centuries, and in early times, when these great mammals remained free from human predation, they must have numbered in their tens of thousands. It appears that the indigenous peoples valued the meat, oil and whalebone which were collected from stranded animals, but did not physically hunt the animals until the mid-17th century.

Although Jan van Riebeeck, leader of the first Dutch settlers at the Cape, made tentative moves to start a whale fishery in the 1650s, it was to be the French and, later, the British and American whalers who really showed the way. By 1791 a fleet of 32 British ships was operating out of St Helena Bay, on the West Coast, and recording catches of about 600 whales a year. The Dutch colonists resented this foreign intrusion and attempted to regulate the nascent industry, but without success. By 1795, just one 'South African' whaling station had been established – in Table Bay – and this, too, proved a failure.

Shore whaling began to expand after 1806, when factories made their appearance in Kalk Bay, Simon's Town and Gordon's Bay on the Cape Peninsula, St Helena Bay in the west and Mossel Bay and Plettenberg Bay on the south coast. These shore-based establishments employed two to four open boats and between 12 and 45 men. Whalers favoured *Eubalaena australis* over other coastal species because it yielded larger quantities of oil and whalebone, swam slowly, was easy to catch, tended to float when dead and, all in all, was the 'right' whale to catch. Hence its common name. The coastal catch, though small compared with those of the earlier, foreign whalers, was particularly damaging to the right whale population because it consisted for the most part of vulnerable adult females – those which either had dependent young or were about to calve.

By the 1830s it was quite clear to everyone that southern right whales were becoming scarcer by the year. Some of the whaling enterprises were closed, but others found it profitable enough to carry on, for just one carcass yielded enough income to support the crews and maintain equipment. Late in the 19th century the catch was occasionally supplemented with the humpback species.

And by 1878 the era of modern whaling, ushered in by the harpoon cannon mounted on a steamer, had begun.

THE TWENTIETH
CENTURY SCENE

The South African Whaling Company was established in Durban in 1907, at which time the first whale was caught by the new method; by 1913 there were 11 floating factories and 17 land stations operating between Gabon (in West Africa) and central Mozambique in the east, and in that year alone, an estimated 10 135 whales were taken from the coast of southern Africa – an unsustainable figure. Between 1914 and 1930 fin and blue whales dominated the catch, though many sperm whales were also taken. Walvis Bay, on the coast of what is today Namibia, appeared to be an area where especially large and fat blue whales could be found (one specimen measured 27.7 m in length and produced 48.8 tons of oil).

Among the more critical innovations of the 1920s was the stern slipway, through which whales could be hauled onto the ship's deck for processing. Well-organized expeditions were now able to move into Antarctic waters in search of blue whales. In less than three years the number of floating factories in the southern seas leapt from 18 to 41.

Early whaling was a hard and often dangerous business. BELOW: A dramatic incident in Greenland waters, recorded (and somewhat embellished) in a book published in 1836. OPPOSITE, ABOVE: The era of modern whaling arrived with the introduction of the harpoon cannon in the 1870s. OPPOSITE, BELOW: A contemporary harpoon with its detachable, explosive head.

WHY WHALES WERE HUNTED

Originally, these marine mammals were valued for their meat, and for their oil, which was used in household lamps, soaps, ointments and in cooking. Later, during the industrial revolution, whale blubber was melted down to produce a lubricant for machinery.

Whalebone or baleen, a plastic-like material that hangs in plates from the upper jaws of filter-feeding whales, found wide application during the 19th century. It was light, flexible, tough, easily cut into thin strips, and it went into the making of brooms, brushes, umbrellas and anything else that required strength and elasticity.

Baleen was especially sought after by the fashion industry, where it was used in stays for corsets, for skirt hoops, men's stiff shirt-collars and for shoe-horns.

In their idle hours at sea, sailors would carve the teeth (of sperm whales) and bones into ornaments – a now almost forgotten craft known as scrimshaw.

Scenes aboard an American whaler operating in Table Bay around the turn of the century.

International concern began to mount as the industry made savage inroads into the whale populations. In 1931, the League of Nations, sitting in Geneva, produced a Convention for the Regulation of Whaling which, among other things, placed an outright ban on the exploitation of all right whales and of the calves, sexually immature individuals and lactating females of other species. It also called for the calculation of a whaler's bonus according to size, species and oil yield (rather than on number) and maintenance of accurate catch records, which were to be sent to a central bureau in Norway.

Neither Natal nor the Cape Province incorporated any of the provisions of the convention into domestic legislation.

Fortunately, the second world war intervened to reduce whaling activity – and provided a much-needed breathing space in which to negotiate further limits. In 1946 fifteen nations, South Africa among them, signed the new International Agreement for the Regulation of Whaling, which came into effect in 1948 and established an International Whaling Commission (IWC). This embraced many of the requirements of the previous convention but added articles providing for a whaling inspector on each ship; for minimum size restrictions on blue, fin, humpback and sperm whales, and for a three-month season for pelagic (open-sea) hunting of baleen whales south of Latitude 40 degrees south.

Unhappily, though, the IWC initiative failed: the Commission simply could not prevent whaling in Antarctic waters. Moreover, the introduction of permits limiting catches to 'units' based on oil yield, and which did not differentiate one kind of whale from another, made it impossible to restrict the harvesting of particular species. Post-war catches of fin whales increased dramatically; no fewer than 305 000 of the animals were taken in the seasons after 1946, and their availability declined by a huge 80 per cent.

In response, South African companies intensified their search for new whale stocks, setting their sights on sei and sperm whales. In 1966 the sei catches dropped dramatically, which proved catastrophic for South African whaling stations in Durban and Donkergat (Langebaan) on the West Coast.

Before 1962, only small numbers of sperm whales had been caught in the southern hemisphere north of 40 °S, even though the hunting of this species had never been prohibited. In that year, however, some fleets came across large numbers of them in transit to and from the Antarctic, and the haul included a large number of females – despite a minimum size limit that should have ensured their protection.

And then, in 1968, the whaling nations began to target minke whales, smallest of the baleens (they grow to a mere 10 metres or so). But minke catches at Durban never exceeded 200 per year, and proved an inadequate substitute for the loss of the sei and fin whale harvests.

In desperation, one company even began to hunt killer whales (36 were taken between 1971 and 1975). Something, obviously, had to be done to save what remained of perhaps the most valuable of all marine resources.

Solutions were forced on the authorities: the diminishing whale populations and, after 1973, huge hikes in the price of fuel finally brought an end to a 184-year period of virtually uninterrupted whaling off southern Africa's coasts. In 1979, the South African government expanded regulations, under the Sea Fisheries Act, to prohibit any person from involvement with any factory, ship or fishing boat used for the freezing or processing of whales, and from supplying goods for use on whaling vessels.

And now the whales are back. Southern rights, in particular, have been increasing in number at an annual rate of about 7 per cent which, if the pace is maintained, will double the population every ten years. In 1995, the southern ocean was home to 2 000 individuals out of a world total of some 5 000.

A scale model, accurate to the last detail, of an American East Coast whaler of the mid-19th century.

All About Whales

Every single one of the earth's marine mammals has evolved from land creatures which, at different times over the past 60 million years, returned to the seas. This was an extraordinary evolutionary process, demanding radical changes to the structure and workings of the animals' bodies and to their behaviour.

Recent theories suggest that all whales and dolphins, or cetaceans, evolved from the same line as pigs, camels, antelope, cattle and the hippopotamus, although this is by no means certain. Seal evolution is also the subject of scientific debate, but it is probable that they originated in inland waters and thus, to some degree, have remained bound to land. It seems that the sirenians – dugongs and manatees – developed from the same group that produced the elephants and dassies (hyraxes, or rock rabbits).

The first of what we would recognize as whale-like species lived about 40 million years ago but, although highly adapted to life in the oceans, they were very different from modern cetaceans. They were large, about 15 m long, with flattened, fish-like tails quite unlike the flukes of modern whales. The teeth of these ancient animals, or rather, the arrangement of their teeth, were similar in some respects to those of humans – that is, they had molars and incisors.

WHALE TYPES

The two main groups into which whales are divided are the baleen whales and the toothed whales.

Baleen whales feed on minute planktonic organisms such as krill and copepods, which they sieve from the water through the baleen plates hanging from the roofs of their mouths. Among the baleens of the southern oceans are the southern right, the

A humpback whale 'lobtailing'. The motivation for this behavioural habit is not entirely clear, but the display could signal either alarm or irritation, or both.

pygmy right, the humpback and – largest of all animals – the 30-m long blue whale.

The toothed whales hunt a variety of marine prey, including squid, octopus, fish and seabirds. The killer whale (the orca) preys on other marine mammals. Among the other toothed whales of southern regions are the beaked species (family Ziphiidae), the great sperm whale and the pygmy sperm whale.

PATTERNS OF BEHAVIOUR

Whales have a number of physical habits of behaviour that are quite distinctive, and clearly discernible to human observers.

Blowing (or spouting): air is expelled from the lungs through the blowhole, which produces a hollow, echoing sound and a spout of vapour (a mix of sea-water and condensation from the animal's hot breath). One can often identify the species from the spout's shape (the southern right's forms a distinctive 'V'), but much depends on weather conditions: visibility needs to be good if not perfect.

Breaching: the most spectacular of whale habits. The animal will sometimes thrust almost its entire body out of the water in a massive, oddly graceful leap to fall back with a great splash. The reasons are not clear; the behaviour may be related to a communication process or to aggressive display; probably helps in the moulting process, and in getting rid of whale lice. On the other hand it may simply express joyfulness.

Grunting: a resonant bellow, which can be heard 2 km away and, at that distance, sounds like a protracted moan. Often uttered at night.

Lobtailing: a whale will raise its tail and slap the water hard: probably a signal of some sort; a sign of alarm or annoyance. Often seen in mothers with calves.

Sailing: the tail is raised and kept vertical for long periods; possibly a means of temperature control; possibly a pose adopted when feeding on organisms just below the surface; possibly just plain exhibitionism.

Spyhopping: some whales, including the southern right, lift their head above the water and appear to be observing what's happening on the surface – which is exactly what they're doing. Cetaceans have well-developed eyesight, able to focus both beneath and above the surface.

THE SENSES OF MARINE MAMMALS

All animals rely on one or more of the five common senses, namely taste, smell, touch, sight and hearing, for information about their surroundings. There are also a number of other senses, such as awareness of the earth's magnetic field (relevant to long-distance migration) and sensitivity to electrical current and to tiny changes in sea temperature, that are complex and poorly understood.

Taste and smell are the least developed since they evolved on land and have little use underwater. Cetaceans have retained their taste buds, however, and are probably able to distinguish the quality of water. These faculties are more acute in seals.

Touch. Marine mammals are as touch-sensitive as their terrestrial cousins. Seals and dugongs have whiskers which, in the case of the former, receive vibrations and indicate the size, speed and direction of the surrounding fish. Humpback, southern right and some other whales have hairs, around jaws and blowhole, which are thought to serve the same purposes.

Marine mammals are hunted by sharks (one species, the 'cookie shark', seems to live entirely on whale and dolphin blubber); many of them bear savage scars, and encounters must be extremely painful – but the animals have no limbs, no way of shielding themselves, and they simply have to grin and bear it. Nor can they do much about various irritating parasites. Whale lice, for example, cling to (and eat) the skin around the mouth, blowhole and genitals with specially adapted hooked feet.

Eyesight. Marine mammals have adapted to the underwater dimness in two ways: their eyes have developed to receive more light; and they have evolved echolocation – the ability to gain information about their surroundings by beaming sounds and interpreting the echoes (see Echolocation below).

Hearing. Ears function in the same way as those of land mammals, though the external organs are much reduced or have disappeared altogether. Special adaptations of the sinuses, and echolocation, enable whales and dolphins to judge direction.

Echolocation. Marine mammals make many sounds, from the 'barking' of Cape fur seals to the 'whistling' of a dolphin and the 'singing' of whales. Dolphins and toothed whales also produce brief blasts of high-pitched clicks repeated many times a second, and use the echoes that are bounced back from both stationary and moving objects to 'see' (or rather, to hear) and form a picture of what's around them. Seals may also enjoy this ability. Baleen whales, which have a different skull structure from their toothed cousins, do not produce clicks, though they will be aware of echoes from their own special voice patterns. The faculty, of course, is more important to the toothed animals, which are predators that hunt in the murky waters where eyesight is of limited value.

WHALE AND DOLPHIN 'LANGUAGE'

Seals communicate with each other. So do dugongs. Humpback whales 'sing', and their songs are varied enough for individuals

BREACHING

LOBTAILING

SAILING

SPYHOPPING

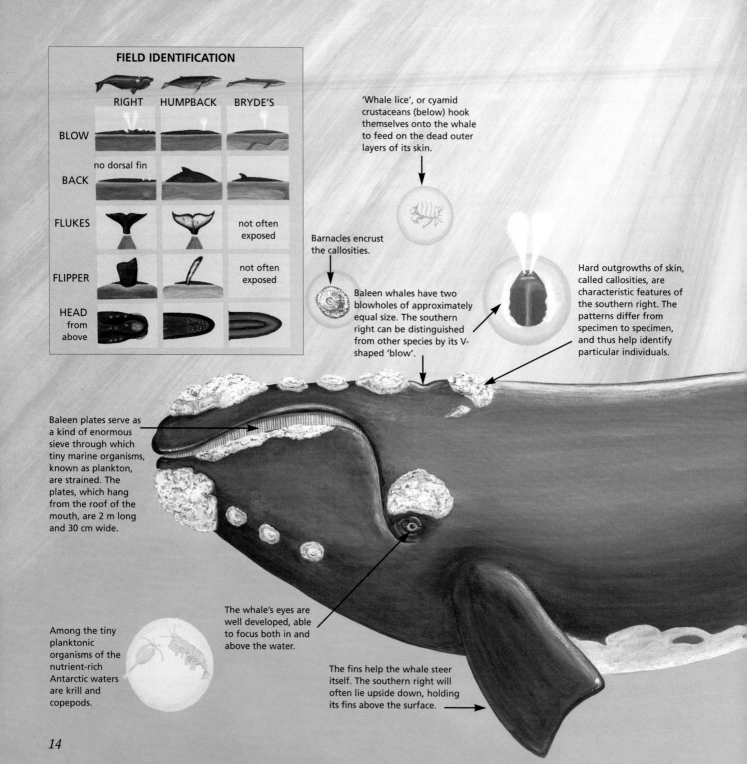

FIELD IDENTIFICATION

	RIGHT	HUMPBACK	BRYDE'S
BLOW			
BACK	no dorsal fin		
FLUKES			not often exposed
FLIPPER			not often exposed
HEAD from above			

'Whale lice', or cyamid crustaceans (below) hook themselves onto the whale to feed on the dead outer layers of its skin.

Barnacles encrust the callosities.

Baleen whales have two blowholes of approximately equal size. The southern right can be distinguished from other species by its V-shaped 'blow'.

Hard outgrowths of skin, called callosities, are characteristic features of the southern right. The patterns differ from specimen to specimen, and thus help identify particular individuals.

Baleen plates serve as a kind of enormous sieve through which tiny marine organisms, known as plankton, are strained. The plates, which hang from the roof of the mouth, are 2 m long and 30 cm wide.

Among the tiny planktonic organisms of the nutrient-rich Antarctic waters are krill and copepods.

The whale's eyes are well developed, able to focus both in and above the water.

The fins help the whale steer itself. The southern right will often lie upside down, holding its fins above the surface.

14

MARINE MAMMALS: FACTS AND FIGURES

◆ Forty-four different kinds of marine mammal are found in southern African waters.

◆ Southern right calves, up to 6 m long when born, consume about 600 litres of milk, and grow 2.8 cm, each day. On average, females produce one calf every three years. Four per cent of the calves are white when born, eventually turning to grey.

◆ Humpback whales were the first to be hunted by modern methods – canon-fired harpoons – in southern African waters. Between 1908 and 1925 about 25 000 were killed. Protected since 1963, they are making a rapid recovery.

◆ Probably the longest of southern cetacean migrations is that of the humpback whale, which moves between its Antarctic feeding grounds and its breeding areas in the tropics.

◆ Southern rights have a top speed of 17 km/h, but usually move at a modest rate of between 0.5 and 4 km/h. Their maximum diving depth is about 300 m. Lifespan unknown, but in excess of 50 years.

◆ Southern rights are recognizable, as individuals, from the patterns of callosities – patches of thickened skin – on their heads.

◆ The southern right population, almost wiped out by whalers over two centuries ago, recovered and the number off southern Africa's coasts, estimated at 1 700 in the mid-1990s, is doubling every ten years.

◆ Nearly 6 million people worldwide are active whale-watchers. Less than 1 per cent of them visit southern Africa.

The southern right whale is up to 800 times heavier than the average (75-kg) man.

The whale's tail flukes serve the same purpose as the scuba-diver's flippers, propelling the body through the water. The southern right will sometimes raise its flukes above the surface, a habit known as 'lobtailing'.

THE SOUTHERN RIGHT WHALE

This large (up to 60-tonne) baleen species is the most common of the whales seen off southern Africa's coasts. Early whalers considered it the 'right' whale to catch because it moved slowly enough for rowing boats to approach, its carcass floated, and it produced high yields of oil and baleen.

15

to be recognized. It has been suggested that whale sounds travel hundreds of kilometres beneath the sea and represent 'long-distance calls' to each other. Dolphins emit an array of different sounds, which must serve as some sort of communication.

Does all this, or any of it, amount to 'language'? Nobody knows: the subject is under scientific investigation, but up to now no firm evidence has come to light of a level of communication beyond that of other social animals.

INTELLIGENCE

Legend and literature are filled with tales of the dolphin's intelligence and its affinity with humankind. Indeed there are many documented instances of dolphins rescuing people from danger. One such case was that of Yvonne Vladislowich, who was saved from certain death off the east coast when two dolphins held her above the water and guided her to a buoy, to which she clung until help arrived. On other occasions the animals have physically extricated a drowning person from the depths, gently and firmly pushing him or her to the surface – which is precisely how a mother dolphin helps her newborn baby take its first lungful of air. Nor is this affinity confined to rescue. The dolphins off Laguna, a small Brazilian coastal town, regularly and deliberately herd shoals of fish into the fishermen's nets. The dolphin's sometimes almost uncanny ability to learn and perform can be seen in oceanariums throughout the world.

Dolphins have large brains – a bottlenose's is about one-and-a-half times the size of a man's. But there needs to be much more research before we know just how intelligent marine mammals are, and the precise nature of that intelligence.

A bottlenose dolphin leaps clear of the water. This and other species also delight in riding the bow-waves of boats – seemingly for sheer pleasure, in reality (it is thought) as a means of conserving energy.

Namibia and Namaqualand

Southern Africa's western seaboard, from the Kunene River in northern Namibia to South Africa's Olifants River, is among the earth's most desolate. And no stretch is more forbidding than the Skeleton Coast, graveyard of a thousand ships and named for the many mariners who, over the centuries, survived the wrecks only to perish in the wastes of the hinterland. Unique in its savage beauty, it is today embraced within a protected area.

The Skeleton Coast Park is a slender strip of drifting sand, gravel flat, canyon and jagged dolorite dyke that runs from the Kunene southwards for 600 km. Its shoreline is especially intimidating, a compound of beaches littered with the bones of birds, seals and dolphins, hidden reefs, fog-shrouded outcrops and sudden sand-bars pounded by the violence of a sea angered by wind and treacherous crosscurrent. Here, in this empty, arid, hostile land, there is naught for the comfort of man.

Yet, astonishingly, this coastal region does have its living forms, flora and fauna which are superbly adapted and often unique to the environment. Most of the plants and insects depend for their moisture on the thick mists that sweep in from the ocean; black-backed jackals have learnt to subsist on what they can glean from the storm-battered beaches; inland, along the northern edges of the wilderness, there is underground water that sustains larger animals, among them elephant, zebra, lion and a variety of antelope.

The park's southern limit is the Ugab River; the terrain to the south is somewhat less hostile, its seaboard part of the National West Coast Tourist Recreation Area. A fairly good road (it has a hard, salty surface) takes you from Swakopmund to Torra Bay, where there is a camping and caravan site, and on to Terrace Bay (shop; restaurant; rooms for hire). Among the major areas of interest along this southern stretch is the Cape Cross Seal Reserve, whose rocky shoreline serves as home to up to 100 000 Cape fur seals (and as a staging post for great numbers of cormorants on their way between roosting and feeding grounds). The bull seals begin to establish their territories and attract their harems around the middle of October; the pups are born towards the end of November and in early December.

SHORES OF THE NAMIB

Namibia's long coastline is, if not featureless, remarkably free of promontories, embayments and natural harbours, and this evenness, together with the harsh nature of the hinterland, has discouraged development. In fact there are only four urban centres of any

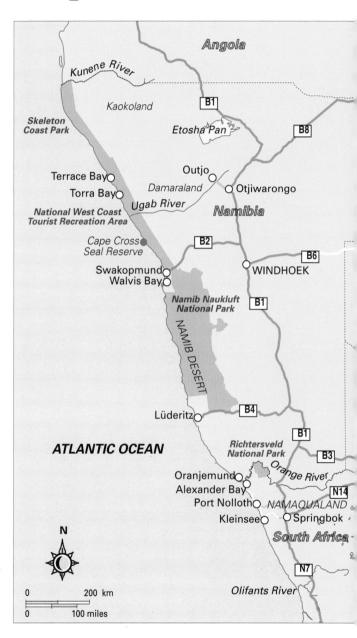

TOP: *The graphic Ugab gateway to Namibia's desolate Skeleton Coast Park.* CENTRE: *Anglers cast their lines near Swakopmund.* ABOVE: *Pleasant colonial-style buildings in Lüderitz.* ABOVE RIGHT: *On safari in the sandy wastes of the Namib-Naukluft Park.*

significance along the entire 1 495-km maritime belt, and one of them owes its existence not to the sea but to the wealth that lies in, and sometimes on, the arid land.

Swakopmund, the northernmost, is a substantial residential town and the country's premier seaside resort. It is surrounded by desert sands that are sometimes whipped to a frenzy by strong easterly winds, and the waters of the ocean are usually too chilly for comfortable bathing (though the surfing is excellent), but for the rest it remains a pleasant enough venue for the tourist and holiday-maker: it has a fine beach, a sheltered swimming area, Olympic-sized heated pool, an 18-hole golf course, museum (natural history), enticing restaurants (German food a speciality) and some interesting colonial architecture. The nearby salt pans sustain a myriad coastal and aquatic birds.

Bird life is even more prolific, though, around Swakopmund's neighbour Walvis Bay, 32 km to the south. Here the lagoon, the reed-filled marshes of Bird Island, and Sandwich Bay down the coast, host enormous concourses of flamingos, pelicans, terns and others; at times more than half a million individuals (belonging to anything up to 120 species) can be seen within the latter area.

Walvis Bay and Lüderitz, far down the Namib seaboard, are the country's main ports, their economies based largely on the fishing industry and on mineral exports. Lüderitz, like Swakopmund, also has its colonial charm and its museum (worth visiting for the Khoisan exhibits); of interest is Dias Point, where there is a replica of a *padrao*, or cross, erected by the path-finding navigator in 1487; and nearby Halifax Island, a penguin sanctuary. Lüderitz, founded in the 1860s as a prelude to German colonization, became a thriving mining village after the discovery of diamonds in 1908. It still serves the diggings, but today the industry's focus is much farther south, at Oranjemund close to the Orange River, the Namibia-South Africa border. Oranjemund, exclusively a diamond mining 'company town' set a little way inland and 8 km from the estuary, is a surprisingly refreshing place of tree-lined streets, parks and neat suburban gardens – a floral richness nurtured by the waters of the river. Security here is strict; visitors may only enter with permission.

All four centres are desert towns, remote, enveloped in the vastness of the Namib, the coasts between them a sailor's hell of high wind, submarine rock, tide-race and unpredictable current that have also claimed their victims. Inland is a sea of sand where rank upon rank of massive, shifting dunes, some of them 250 m high and fully 30 km long, march to distant horizons – a bone-dry wasteland of searingly hot days and often bitter nights, of solitude and an immense silence. Yet it too has its plants and animals. Most of these are highly specialized; some, notably the beetles and the sand-burrowing lizards, are found nowhere else, for the Namib is the earth's oldest desert, and the long millennia have given free reign to the evolutionary process.

NAMAQUALAND

South of the Orange lies Namaqualand, a 48 000-km² region whose southern extremity is the mouth of the Olifants River. The coastal strip is classed as sandveld, narrow for the most part, elevated above sea level and distinguished by what are known as 'raised beaches' – terraces full of seashells and wave-eroded pebbles that hark back to that far-distant period when the ocean's surface was about 100 m higher than it is today.

Namaqualand's 'capital' is Springbok, a sleepy little inland town set astride the main highway (the N7). Rather more lively are the two coastal centres of Alexander Bay and Port Nolloth, both fishing ports and, latterly, products of a diamond industry launched when Jack Carstens stumbled across the first glittering stone in 1925. Prospectors flocked to the barren, 80-km 'diamond strip' along the northern seaboard to make their fortunes; some were lucky, a few became wealthy overnight, but conditions became chaotic and the diggings were eventually taken over by the state.

Alexander Bay, close to the Orange River in the far north, is the hub of the country's alluvial (sea, beach and land) fields and, although this too is a 'closed' town, the mining company welcomes, even encourages visitors. And its operations, from the time

The glory of Namaqualand's desert flowers. Most of the region's flora belong to the daisy and mesembryanthemum families.

The best place to see whales and dolphins is in the Swakopmund area. Cape fur seals are common along the entire western seaboard as far north as Cape Frio near the Kunene River mouth (the biggest concentration is at Cape Cross). More specifically, one can see:

♦ Southern rights (below) in most bays during winter. Less common, but visible from promontories, are Bryde's and humpback and, occasionally (though these are deeper water creatures), minke whales.

♦ Killer whales from Cape Point northwards into Namibia; most sightings are between Lüderitz and Walvis Bay.
♦ Dolphins: dusky and Heaviside's from Cape Town northwards into Namibia. Bottlenose dolphins from Lambert's Bay northwards. They are often seen as close as 15 m from beaches.

For information, call the MTN Whale Hotline on 083 910 1028.

Namaqualand's countryside takes on its brief springtime beauty.

when colossal earthmovers slice away great chunks of the ground to the sifting process, are certainly worth seeing. To the south is Port Nolloth, originally established to serve the copper mines of the area but today more preoccupied with diamonds and the fruits of the sea. These towns are linked to each other and to Springbok by road; there's a good gravel route between Port Nolloth and Kleinsee to the south (though this is a prohibited area); communications along the rest of the Namaqualand coast range from the rugged to the nonexistant. Not that there is much to attract the sightseeing traveller: this is a bleak enough shoreline, notable mainly for its seabirds, seals and, sometimes, the whales in the offshore waters. Among the few settlements of substance is Hondeklip Bay, which you get to along the inland route.

Indeed, pretty well the whole of Namaqualand is arid and sparsely populated. It has very little surface water; rainfall varies between 250 mm and a pitiful 50 mm a year, and for the most part the harsh terrain seems capable of supporting only the hardiest forms of life. But its soils, and especially the coastal sandveld, are home to a huge profusion of succulents and flowering plants – an astonishing 4 000 and more species in all. Most are daisies and mesembryanthemums of one sort or another. Small, low-growing and drought-resistant, their seeds lie dormant during the long dry months and then, after the modest winter rains and before the onset of the desert breezes, when the earth becomes warm and the pollinators are abroad, they burst into sudden life. In springtime, in the brief few weeks after about mid-September, the countryside is mantled in great, glorious carpets of blooms.

The West Coast

The coast that runs north from Cape Town is scenically rather bare, and there is little to draw the eye among the deserted, windswept stretches of beach, the low dunes and their backing of treeless sandveld. But the region has something special about it, a silence, an uncluttered simplicity, a sense of space that sweeps the mind of its distractions and lifts the spirit.

And there is much of specific interest. The Atlantic waters, cooled by the Benguela current that sweeps up from the Antarctic, yield a major portion of South Africa's fishing bounty, sustaining a number of pretty little coastal villages and drawing keen anglers to the shores. Others come to catch, and savour, the crayfish (rock lobsters) that thrive among the kelp beds, reefs and rocky shelves.

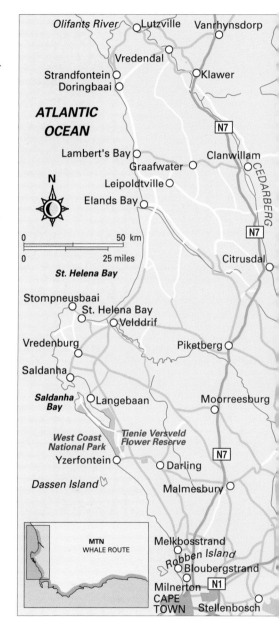

Whales, southern rights for the most part, are regular visitors to the bays of the West Coast between June and December; less often seen are the humpbacks, which begin to arrive in May on their long journey from the Antarctic to Angolan waters, and (though they are much more common in the east) the normally deeper-water Bryde's whale occasionally comes close enough inshore to be observed from cliff or beach. Dolphin species include the common, the bottlenose, Heaviside's and the dusky.

The region is also something of a paradise for the bird-watcher: the seaboard and its offshore islands host numerous seabirds – cormorants, gannets, gulls and many others – that often gather in colonies so dense that there's hardly a wingspan of open space in the great, roosting concourses.

And then there are the wild flowers. The springtime glory is by no means confined to the desolate plains of Namaqualand: for a few weeks each year bright carpets also mantle the land south of the Olifants River, patchwork profusions of daisies and other ephemeral plants that add colour and grace to the countryside.

Two roads lead north from Cape Town, one of which – the main N7 highway – runs inland, with lesser routes leading off to the various coastal destinations. In its first (150-km) stretch it takes you through the wheatland expanses of what is known as the Swartland, or 'black country', so named for the rich darkness of its soil. Perhaps other colours, however, would be more appropriate, for in spring the countryside is bright green with the splendid harvests, and in summer a ripe gold. Here, too, there are pastures and vineyards, fields of vegetables and orchards heavy with fruit.

Malmesbury, founded in 1743 in the shallow valley of the Diep River, is the 'capital' of the Swartland; other centres include Mooreesburg (noted for its wheat museum, one of only three such in the world) and Piketberg. Drive farther north and you'll enter the immensely fertile Olifants River valley, known for its citrus groves, its rooibos tea industry and for the pleasant little towns of Citrusdal and Clanwilliam. Just to the east are the high mountains of the Cedarberg, a ruggedly beautiful wilderness area of strangely eroded rock formations, of waterfalls, crystal streams and clear pools, of caverns, overhangs, peaks, deep ravines and magnificent viewsites.

The second route north hugs the coast for much of the way, the journey taking you, for the most part, along the R27.

ABOVE: Cape gannets gather in huge breeding colonies on the cliffs and, especially, the offshore islands of the West Coast. OPPOSITE, LEFT: Looking south from Bloubergstrand to Table Mountain.

There's good whale-watching over the first stretch, which embraces Bloubergstrand (superb views of distant Table Mountain, and some fine restaurants), Melkbosstrand, the Koeberg Nature Reserve (near the nuclear power station; conducted tours are laid on) and Silverstroom, a wide beach made for strolling.

YZERFONTEIN

This tiny fishing village, 80 km from Cape Town, comes to life in the busy (winter) snoek season, when the salt-stained working boats chug in to offload their catches, and the gulls wheel around in frenzied anticipation. Southern rights can be viewed from a number of sites; locals and visiting guests complain they're kept awake at night by the moans and squeals of these massive marine mammals. Keep a lookout, too, for the common dolphin and the triangular dorsal fin of the Heaviside's dolphin which, if you're out on a boat trip, might ride the bow-waves.

From the headland you get a clear view of the bay and its minuscule harbour, of the white beaches that sprawl away to the north, of nearby Meeurots (gull rock), and of Dassen Island to the southwest.

The latter is the largest of the the 40 or so small, submerged mountains off southern Africa's south and west coasts whose summits, projecting above the ocean surface, are large enough to be termed islands and which are inhabited by multitudes of seabirds. They are collectively known as the Guano Islands for their enormous deposits of bird droppings – a valuable source of fertilizer and focus of the 19th-century 'guano wars'

IN SEARCH OF WILD FLOWERS

The West Coast's lovely wild-flower displays are usually at their most eye-catching during the three weeks after mid-September, but this varies from year to year and place to place according to the subtle interplay of temperature, rainfall and wind. August can also be rewarding. For the most up-to-date information, telephone or call in at The Tourism Gateway Centre, Cape Town, or contact the regional tourism office (see page 102).

Among the most impressive shows are those in the Postberg section of the West Coast National Park; in the Darling, Vanrhynsdorp, Lamberts Bay and Strandfontein areas and, inland, around Nieuwoudtville and in the exquisite Biedouw Valley to the north of the Cedarberg range.

The flowers open only on bright days, their faces turning to and following the sun on its course. Thus the viewing period is between ten in the morning and late afternoon. Stand with your back to the sun.

Numerous flower tours are laid on in season, ranging from day trips to longer journeys that take in many other points of interest. Traditional West Coast meals, which focus on seafood, are a feature of the excursions.

Many visitors prefer to arrange their own itineraries. If you intend touring for more than a day, consider private accommodation – on a farmstead, for instance – as an attractive alternative to hotel booking, especially in the remoter areas. Details from West Coast Tourism or the The Tourism Gateway (see Useful Contacts, page 102).

Jackass penguins on Dassen Island. This bird, whose name derives from its harsh, donkey-like call, is southern Africa's only resident member of the penguin family.

between competing commercial interests. Dassen is 223 hectares in extent and, although it rises just 10 m above sea level at its highest point, serves as the main breeding ground of the jackass penguin. Nearly 100 000 of these vulnerable birds congregate here in September, and again in February. Also among the island's residents are other seabird species, tortoises and rock rabbits (hyraxes) or 'dassies', which gave the place its name.

LANGEBAAN

The village, about 40 km farther up the coast from Yzerfontein, lies at the mouth of a long (16-km), narrow lagoon that projects inland as an arm of Saldanha Bay. It is the focal point of a magnificent wetland wilderness area that, in turn, forms part of the relatively new West Coast National Park.

This was once an important whaling area (especially to the 18th and 19th century 'Yankee Whalers'). John Bryde opened a station at Donkergat in 1909, his three whale-catchers leading South Africa into the industry's modern era. Shortly afterwards another station opened at Salamander Bay, and both prospered for a time. But by the 1960s the seas had been plundered of their wealth and the whales came no more. Now, with the international moratorium in place, they are returning in growing numbers.

WATCH FOR...
◆ Southern right whales, though they are less common in the west than along the southern coasts.
◆ Killer whales (orcas). These animals occur in both coastal and deep waters, but sightings are irregular.
◆ Heaviside's dolphins: again, sightings tend to be a matter of luck; said to be especially common in the Lambert's Bay area.
◆ Dusky dolphins are opportunistic visitors.
◆ Common dolphins call occasionally; St Helena Bay is said to yield more sightings than most.
◆ Cape fur seals: anywhere along the coasts, though mostly confined to rookeries on the offshore islands.

For information, call the MTN Whale Hotline on 083 910 1028.

The Mediterranean-style apartment buildings of Club Mykonos, the West Coast's largest and most lively resort complex. It lies on the northern shores of Langebaan Lagoon.

Although the whales seldom enter the lagoon – the water is too shallow – you can observe them from various points on the park's flanking coast, the best perhaps those at Sixteen Mile Beach and Plankiesbaai. Best time to view: August and September. Sometimes, southern rights will also brave the waters off Club Mykonos, a large and busy hotel, timeshare and resort complex just to the north. The place is well worth a visit for its other attractions: drawing its design inspiration from the Greek isles, it features whitewashed, colourfully trimmed Mediterranean-style buildings, cobbled alleys and village squares; shops, restaurants, pubs, coffee houses, delicatessans, boutiques, a health centre, a marina and all the sporting facilities you could wish for.

Langebaan Lagoon, the area's salt marshes, the mud- and sand-banks and the rocky shores and islands of Saldanha Bay are a magnet for a myriad waders and other bird species – flamingos, cormorants, plovers, gulls, gannets, herons, knots, turnstones, sacred ibis and, most numerous, curlew sandpipers. Altogether, there are about 60 000 birds in residence during the summer months. Most migrate from breeding grounds in the Arctic and sub-Arctic regions, embarking on their long and often final flight to the sunny south in August. All are attracted to Langebaan by its rich abundance of nutrients: marine algae, tiny snails and other mud-loving organisms.

THE SALDANHA AREA

Beyond Langebaan is the broad expanse of Saldanha Bay, which, though one of the southern hemisphere's finest natural harbours, remained undeveloped for centuries because it lacked fresh water. Today, however, the area is a prime growth point: it serves as the headquarters of the West Coast's fishing industry, as a deep-sea terminal for the export of iron ore, and site of a giant new steel-making enterprise. The town itself has the full range of visitor amenities.

The islands of the bay – Malgas, Jutten, Marcus and Schaapen – are rich in bird life, home to gannets, jackass penguins, cormorants and others. Schaapen hosts southern Africa's largest colony of kelp gulls. One can visit (but not land on) the islands by boat; charter facilities are on offer at the harbour. For whale-watchers, Saldanha Bay's best viewing site is the 1.8-km long causeway that links Marcus Island to the mainland.

Just to the north of Saldanha is St Helena Bay, 'discovered' by Vasco da Gama in 1497 and now given over largely to commercial fishing. The waters here yield huge quantities of pilchards, anchovies, mackerel and other species; the shores are dotted with tiny coastal villages and rather ugly fish factories. But there is beauty too – in the meeting of dark-blue sea and bone-white rock, and in the lovely mosaic of wheatfields and pastures that grace the immediate hinterland.

Among the area's best whale-watching spots are the village and surrounds of Stompneusbaai (where there's a monument to Da Gama's landfall on that far-off November day) and Britannia Bay, both on the headland that guards the western end of St Helena Bay. To the south is Paternoster, a charming hamlet that takes its name from the heartfelt prayer of thanksgiving offered up by a party of early shipwreck survivors. Nearby Cape Columbine is a joy in the wild-flower season. This stretch of the coast has witnessed two mass whale strandings in fairly recent years.

ELANDS BAY

The coastal road leads you through arid-looking terrain, the monotony relieved by the popular Dwarskersbos resort and, here and there, by marshy patches and a series of lagoons (known as Die Vlei) that are, literally, oases in the wilderness. They are also a paradise for wildfowl and waders. For the rest, there's little else for the eye to take in except the immensity of sea and sky – and, in season, the sight of southern rights frolicking with their young just beyond the waves.

Farther north, beyond the bird-rich Rocher Pan, is Elands Bay, set at the mouth of Verlorenvlei and much favoured by the quieter kind of weekender for its beach, and by the surfer for the magnificent 'tubes' that break when the southeaster blows up a swell. The Verlorenvlei estuary is the largest along the entire West Coast and, although the water is saline, it serves as a fine breeding ground for multitudes of pelicans, herons, egrets, flamingos, geese, ducks, moorhens, purple gallinules and a host of summer migrants – some 240 bird species altogether.

The cliffs of Baboon Point, on the south side of the estuary, provide an excellent lookout for whale-watchers. Here, too, there is a spacious cave which provided shelter for generations of prehistoric folk. Its walls are embellished with their art; its floor is deep in shells – testament to the lengthy occupancy of those long-gone people.

LAMBERT'S BAY

This picturesque little fishing town is the headquarters of the country's crayfish (rock lobster) industry which, apart from filling the local coffers, attracts a steady stream of summertime gourmets. Whale-spotters also visit in season to observe the southern rights and humpbacks (small but growing numbers migrate into the area between May

WINES OF THE WEST COAST
Some excellent wines are produced in the western areas. Indeed the Swartland has twice produced the national champion white. Several co-operatives and estates have come together to form the Swartland wine route; wine cellars include Swartland (just outside Malmesbury), the Riebeeck (Riebeeck Kasteel area: its Chenin Blanc won the 1985 national award), the Mamreweg; the Winkelshoek; the Porterville; the Cedarberg, where you can buy, among other things, fine vintages produced on the Nieuwoudt family farm; and the renowned Allesverloren estate (visits by appointment). The Vredendal cellars offer a wide range of dessert labels and the local 'witblits', a fierce, pale, brandy-type brew.

A similar route has been established in the Olifants River valley to the north – it stretches from Citrusdal to Lutzville; Vredendal boasts the country's largest winery under one roof; the Klawer cellar has won an international gold medal for its Blanc de Noir.

For details, contact the Swartland & Sandveld Tourism Association, tel: (0224) 22996; or the Olifants River & West Coast Wine Trust; tel: (0271) 33126.

THE DEATH WISH

Whales that strand themselves along this coast usually do so alone, but on two notable occasions whole schools have beached on the shores of St Helena Bay: one in 1936, the second in 1981. Altogether, 123 of the animals perished.

In both cases they were false killer whales, but other species also come ashore to die – and just why they do so remains a mystery. It may be because, for some poorly understood reason, an animal's navigation system breaks down. Or, in St Helena's case, the topography may have confused the creature. But there is probably a lot more to it than that, for beached whales sometimes resist rescue, heading straight back to shore after being refloated.

If you happen to witness such a stranding, get in touch with the MTN Centre for Dolphin Studies (see page 102) or the MTN Whale Hotline on 083 910 1028. And, while you're waiting, round up as many people as you can to keep the animal cool and moist – but make certain no water finds its way down the animal's blowhole as this leads directly to its lungs.

Tough little fishing boats at rest on the still harbour waters of St Helena Bay. Pilchards, anchovies and mackerel are among the main catches.

and December). Bottlenose and Heaviside's dolphins are present the year round, and there have been many reports of killer whale sightings over the years. All can be viewed either from the shore or on boat trips. And, again, there's plenty for the bird-watching enthusiast. The bay's Bird Island – which is something of a misnomer since you can walk to it along the harbour wall – is haven to a vast colony of Cape gannets.

Lamberts Bay has two comfortable guesthouses, self-catering apartments, and an excellent hotel, which lays on trawler cruises and tours of the local crayfish factory. The Sandveld Museum is worth a brief visit. Other local amenities include the Panorama Park Game Reserve; a pleasant golf course; opportunities for sailing, angling, scuba-diving and horse-riding, and hiking trails that lead you across white dune-country.

STRANDFONTEIN

The little seaside town, an increasingly popular holiday resort, nestles against, and is sheltered from the prevailing southeaster by, the rocks and cliffs of a natural amphitheatre. The coast to either side is flatter, windier, often uncomfortably sand-blown. This is a rewarding spot for surfers, anglers – and whale-watchers. A hiking trail leads south, across a gorge-like valley and a rock-fringed cove called Die Hel, to the tiny village of Doring Bay, which supports a canning factory and its associated diamond-recovery enterprise. Among the bigger centres of the area are Lutzville and Vredendal ('valley of peace'), a short distance inland and notable for the vineyards that bring welcome swathes of greenery to the rather bleak countryside.

The Cape Peninsula

Cape Town's central area, nestled snugly between the looming vastness of Table Mountain and the shores of Table Bay, is at the northern end of the Peninsula, a long, narrow and largely mountainous finger of land that probes southwards for 75 kilometres to the Cape of Good Hope Nature Reserve and Cape Point. In extent, the Peninsula is modest enough – just 620 square kilometres – but it embraces an almost infinite variety of landscapes, the high hills, deep valleys and gentle plains giving way to each other with dramatic suddenness.

Much of the central Peninsula is taken up by a forested and strikingly beautiful highland plateau, an extension of the Table Mountain formation. To either side is coastline, rugged in the west, gentle along False Bay in the east. The two seaboards differ markedly, too, in climate and the nature of their waters. False Bay suffers the full force of the summer southeaster while the western shores remain, for the most part, pleasantly sheltered. The sea off the eastern or 'Indian Ocean' coast is much warmer than that of the western or 'Atlantic' side.

Cape Town, founded in 1652 by a small group of Dutch settlers and long known to seafarers as the 'Tavern of the Seas', is still renowned for its hospitality – though it now attracts a much wider clientele. Indeed it is South Africa's premier holiday and tourist destination, its principal drawcards the colossus of Table Mountain, the lovely countryside and its unique plant life, the beaches and bays, the beauty of the winelands hinterland, the stately mansions of yesteryear, the lively calendar of arts and entertainment, and the myriad eating and drinking places.

For more than three centuries Cape Town owed its prominence and prosperity to its strategic position on the ocean lane halfway between Europe and the East – and to its harbour. Today the latter is rather quieter than it was in the heyday of the steamship, but it remains the country's second biggest (after Durban).

WATERFRONT AND RIVIERA

In recent years the Victoria and Alfred basins, the oldest parts of the harbour, have been transformed into a tourist mecca in a huge and imaginative waterfront redevelopment scheme that borrows ideas from San Francisco's harbour project, from Boston, Vancouver, Sydney and elsewhere – but still manages to retain a character very much its own. The quaysides have been cleaned up, promenades and public squares laid out, a yacht basin built (this replaced an unsightly tank farm), the more colourful of the old dockyard buildings have been converted, and

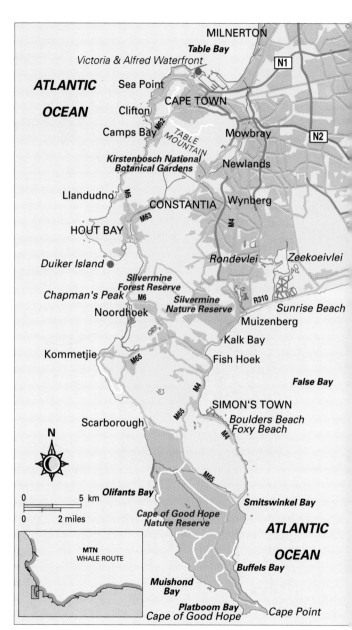

Cape Town's attractive Victoria and Alfred Waterfront, with Table Mountain in the background. The area, oldest part of Table Bay harbour, ranks among the country's top tourist venues.

new ones built, to serve as hotels (some of the country's best), produce and craft markets, restaurants, pubs, umbrella-shaded bistros, cinemas, theatres, speciality shopping complexes, museums (see box).

The Waterfront, though, is not simply a pleasure ground. It remains a working area: the graving dock still functions, salt-stained fishing craft and sturdy tugs move about between the tour boats. Among the trips you can embark on from the Waterfront is that to Robben Island, 10 km offshore, notorious for its role as a maximum-security political prison, and now a nature reserve, museum, and poignant memorial to South Africa's long liberation struggle.

The island was known to and exploited by the earliest white settlers for its marine mammals ('Robben' means 'seals' in Dutch), its penguins, birds' eggs, seashells (used for lime-making) and slate (for building), later serving as livestock pen, later still and at various times as a place for lepers, lunatics, paupers, the chronically sick – and for political prisoners (including high-born exiles from Holland's Far Eastern possessions). Its most recent inmates included Nelson Mandela, first president of the new South Africa.

Cape Town's 'Riviera' extends from the Waterfront and neighbouring Granger Bay along the Peninsula's western coastline for some 8 km, a strip that encompasses the affluent seaside suburbs of Green Point, Sea Point (the shoreline here is rocky), Bantry Bay (a secluded cove), and Clifton and Camps Bay, noted for their superb beaches. Here, the cliffs and hillsides support the homes of the rich (and sometimes famous); beyond, rising splendidly above suburb and sea, is the Lion's Head massif.

HOUT BAY

Victoria Drive follows a virtually deserted and scenically stunning stretch of coastline from the Riviera suburbs to the small, fashionably exclusive seaside village of Llandudno. On your left are the often cloud-wreathed heights of the Twelve Apostles (there are in fact 17 of these towering, sentinel-like peaks); on your right, cliffs that tumble down to boulders and the blue ocean. Picturesque Llandudno, with its rock-flanked little bay and its backing of high mountain, has an especially spectacular setting. Around the promontory to the south is Sandy Bay, a secluded stretch of sand much favoured by sunbathers of the less inhibited kind.

Just over the nek is Hout Bay, a largish and most pleasant harbour town nestling in a wide green valley between mountain and sea. The name means 'Wood Bay', a reference to its value as a source of yellowwood and other timber in early colonial times (the place is still magnificently embowered, but by different and often exotic trees). Today it is an expanding residential area that functions variously as upmarket dormitory settlement, thriving tourist centre and as headquarters of the Peninsula's crayfishing fleet.

Crayfish, though, aren't the only sea harvest: during June and July great quantities of snoek, a large, rather bony and strongly flavoured linefish, are caught offshore (the annual Snoek Festival is held during this period). Hout Bay harbour is one of the region's most attractive, girded around by high mountains, overlooked by the soaring, distinctively shaped Sentinel peak, its waters filled with tough old fishing boats and expensive looking leisure craft.

Whales sometimes enter the bay, coming close inshore. They're more frequently seen, though, in the wider Chapman's Bay (see page 30) beyond.

From Hout Bay, you can embark on a boat trip to nearby Duiker Island where, in the summer months, more than 4 000 Cape fur seals bask on the rocky little islet and frolic in the waters around (they're used to visitors, and tend to show off).

ABOVE RIGHT: Robben Island – once a prison, now a moving memorial and nature reserve. BELOW: Hout Bay and its Sentinel formation (at left), viewed from Chapman's Peak.

WATCH FOR...
◆ Southern right whales: frequent visitors to the Peninsula (both the western and eastern seaboards).
◆ Killer whales (orcas), which occur both in the inshore and the deeper waters; sightings, though, are unpredictable.
◆ Dusky dolphins: opportunistic visitors to bays and inlets; fairly often seen off Fish Hoek and other parts of False Bay, and on the Peninsula's west coast.
◆ Common dolphins are occasionally seen. Heaviside's dolphins: off Cape Point and elsewhere but, again, sightings are a matter of luck. Humpback dolphins may appear close inshore.
◆ Cape fur seals: can be seen anywhere, but Duiker Island, near Hout Bay (boat trips laid on) is the best venue. Also at the V & A Waterfront.

For information, call the MTN Whale Hotline on 083 910 1028.

◆ Mariner's Wharf, at the harbour (below): modelled on its namesake in San Francisco. Fresh fish and lobster market; seafood bistro; excellent restaurant.

◆ The World Of Birds, Africa's largest bird park: walk-through aviaries provide natural habitats for 450 different species.
◆ Hout Bay Museum: local history and environment.
◆ Kronendal, on Main Road: charming 1800s Cape Dutch homestead, now a restaurant.
◆ Excursion inland to Groot Constantia (along the valley, over the hill and down again into the Constantia Valley): grandest of Cape Dutch mansions; wine museum; two restaurants; wine tastings and sales; lovely picnic spots. Turn left at the top of the Hout Bay valley and you'll eventually get to the world-famous gardens of Kirstenbosch, sanctuary for around 9 000 indigenous South African floral species.

CAPE OF GOOD HOPE

The road south continues along Chapman's Peak Drive, a tortuous route cut through multicoloured strata of granite and sandstone of the peak itself. At its highest point the drive skirts cliffs that plunge almost sheer to the bay 600 metres below, and there are breathtaking views from the lookouts and picnic spots along the way – of both Chapman's Bay and Hout Bay. The coastal drive will take you past Noordhoek (noted for its Long Beach and arts-and-crafts route) and, after an inland digression, to Kommetjie and, eventually, to the Cape of Good Hope Nature Reserve (follow the signs), which sprawls across the southern quarter of the Peninsula.

Some 70 km from central Cape Town, the sanctuary covers nearly 8 000 hectares, has a 40-km coastline, and is famed more for its flora – it sustains around 1 200 indigenous flowering plant species with others awaiting the botanists' scrutiny – than its fauna. But the area does have its animals, among them the once-endangered bontebok and other antelope, Cape mountain zebra, Cape fox, and four troops of chacma baboons – thought to be the world's only wild primate group that subsists, largely, on marine resources. The terrain, broken by a ridge running down the eastern (False Bay) side, is crisscrossed by a network of roads and trail paths that lead to viewsites, picnic spots, bays and secluded little beaches. Visitors are free to walk where they wish; there are numerous vantage points for whale-watchers.

The best of the lookouts, and indeed the reserve's principal attraction, is Cape Point itself, the massive headland whose sheer cliffs plunge 300 metres down into the sea. In the often wind-tossed waters far below you can discern shoals of tunny, seals, schools of dolphins and, occasionally, the huge dark shape of a southern right. Around, above and below you gannets, gulls and petrels wheel in noisy profusion.

The purists will assure you that the Atlantic and Indian oceans meet off Cape Agulhas, far to the east (see page 36) but here, at the Point, cold and warm currents merge to produce far more striking effects. There are memorable views from the base of the old lighthouse at the top, which one reaches either on foot, which is only for the fit, or via the funicular (cable car). Cape Point has its place in legend: it is here that the *Flying Dutchman*, a phantom sailing ship with storm-swept decks and tattered sheets, has been sighted on a number of occasions.

FALSE BAY

The bay's warm and often gusty waters lap the whole of the Peninsula's eastern seaboard, its shores fringed by an almost continuous stretch of golden beach and, in the south, by a chain of old-established seaside towns and resort villages linked by rail and coastal road.

For most of the year the sea here is calm enough, attracting anglers, surfers, boating enthusiasts, beach-lovers and, when the southern rights put in an appearance, whale-watchers. But it is not always so benign. Indeed the bay's very name speaks of confusion and danger: it derives from the many occasions when early European navigators mistook Cape Point for Hangklip in the east (see page 33) – an always troublesome and often tragic error, for the winds and currents are perverse and, over the centuries, many a ship has foundered here.

A work-worn fishing boat unloads its morning catch in Kalk Bay harbour, on the Peninsula's east coast. The fish are auctioned on the quayside.

FALSE BAY DESTINATIONS
♦ Simon's Town's museums, including The Residency (built in 1777; contains naval memorabilia); the Stempastorie (national emblems), and the Naval Museum.
♦ Peer's Cave, inland from Fish Hoek: an important prehistoric site, once home to 15 000-year-old Fish Hoek Man.
♦ Kalk Bay harbour, at its busiest and most colourful in the snoek season (June-July).
♦ Natale Labia Museum, Muizenberg: fine furniture, works of art.
♦ Silvermine nature and forest reserve (below), extending across the Peninsula from Muizenberg; a rugged, scenically stunning area; ideal for hiking.
♦ For bird-lovers: Rondevlei Nature Reserve, part of the extensive Cape Flats wetlands.

The most southerly and among the bigger of the coastal centres is Simon's Town, a charming place of steep and cobbled streets. The bay, sheltered from the northwesterly storms by lofty hills, was recommended in 1687 as a safe anchorage by early Cape governor Simon van der Stel and eventually became the Royal Navy's principal South Atlantic base. The South African Navy took over the dockyards in 1957.

Not surprisingly, therefore, naval history mantles the town (among the many notables who spent time here was Horatio Nelson, British admiral and victor of Trafalgar, when he was a lowly midshipman) though there's much else of interest about the place, including several museums and a 'historic mile' embracing 21 venerable buildings of note. To either side of town are attractive beaches and rocky little coves, among them Boulders and Foxy beaches, which support one of only two shore-based colonies of the threatened Cape or jackass penguin.

Farther up the coast are Fish Hoek, a substantial residential centre; Kalk Bay, notable for its eating houses, its antique and craft shops, its charming little harbour and for the raucous fresh-fish auctions held on the quayside; St James, quietly attractive; and Muizenberg, a rather old-fashioned resort town that enjoyed its heyday in Edwardian times, slid into decline and is now making something of a comeback.

Cecil Rhodes lived his last years in Muizenburg – his simple cottage, on the coast road between the town and St James, is now a museum – and loved the place. So too did his friend Rudyard Kipling, who wrote evocatively of the 'white sands of Muizenburg ... spun before the gale'. And indeed the beach is rather special: a huge, wide, gently sloping expanse of fine, pale sand pounded rhythmically by long lines of breakers. It extends eastwards to and beyond Strandfontein; the water along its entire stretch is shallow, safe for bathing, ideal for surfing, board-sailing and yachting. There is especially good whale-viewing along the watchway between Muizenburg and St James, and on scenic Boyes Drive between Kalk Bay and Lakeside.

The Overberg

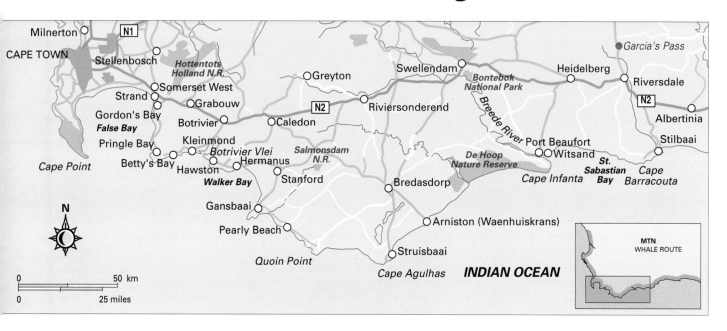

A southern right whale, distinctively marked by the hardened, whitish skin of its callosities, breaks the surface in the Overberg's Walker Bay.

The name Overberg translates as 'over the mountain', which is how the early Dutch residents of Cape Town thought of the lands to the east, beyond the high Hottentots-Holland range. It is a scenically attractive and varied region, known for the rugged cliffs, the embayments and pretty little coves of its shoreline, and for the gentleness of the countryside, its apple orchards, golden fields of wheat, green pastures, forest plantations and the magnificence of its highland rampart.

The ocean here, too, can be gentle, though isn't always so: over the centuries the gales and the currents, and the reefs and jagged rocks of the seashore, have claimed a great many ships. A few of the wrecks can still be seen; the majority are hidden beneath the shallow waters of the great Agulhas Bank. But most days are kinder, the sea placid, warm in summer, and the bays of its shoreline play host to thousands of holiday-makers – and to southern right whales and other cetaceans. For land-based whale-watchers, no other stretch of coast in southern Africa, and few in the world, is as rewarding.

If you glance at the map you'll see that the maritime towns, villages and resorts are rather isolated from each other. There is, for much of the way, a coastal road, but it is rather serpentine and, if you're in a hurry to get to a particular destination, it is probably better to take the N2 national highway from Cape Town, cross over the spectacular Sir Lowry's Pass, and then turn south at the appropriate inland intersection. For the more leisurely whale-spotter, though, the seaboard route is a must.

GORDON'S BAY TO KLEINMOND

Just along the shoreline from Somerset West, nestling at the foot of the high mountains, is the charming, rather upmarket seaside resort village and fishing harbour of Gordon's Bay (it has all the visitor amenities, including a superb hotel). Take the road south, along the eastern flank of False Bay, to Hangklip: the scenery is stunning, and one can occasionally spot whales and their calves in the waters below from both high and low vantage points. The road tends to wind; stick to the designated viewsites.

This part of the False Bay coast is much favoured by serious fishermen, and by those who delight in floral beauty: here, among the hills, one can see magnificent displays of proteas, everlastings and other jewels of the fynbos floral kingdom. Pringle Bay, towards the end of the southward road, is a tranquil and timeless little village whose beach and lagoon entice the more contemplative weekender; Hangklip, at the end, forms the dramatically high southern extremity of the Hottentots-Holland range, a windswept and hauntingly lonely place, once the refuge of runaway slaves and cattle rustlers and now the location of a modest scatter of cottages.

To the west of Hangklip, beyond a trinity of small lakes (they were once river estuaries, long since cut off by the dunes) is Betty's Bay, yet another quiet resort area, whose 190-hectare Harold Porter botanic garden is famed for the wealth and beauty of its indigenous flowers. Here, too, there is an old whaling station, closed down in the 1920s because the plundered ocean could yield little more. The whales are back, though, and at their most visible from Stoney Point. This is also haven – one of only two shore sanctuaries – for the endangered jackass penguin.

Kleinmond, farther along the shoreline to the east, lies near the mouth of the Bot River and at the foot of the 600-metre high Palmietberg; nearby is the Palmiet River lagoon whose waters, and those of Sandown Bay, beckon the fisherman.

HERMANUS

True shore-based southern right whale-spotting country begins at a quartet of alluring little coastal hamlets – Hawston, Vermont, Onrus and Sandbaai – from where, when the northwesterly wind blows, there are frequent sightings in season. But the high cliffs of Hermanus, just beyond, are even more rewarding: they overlook the broad sweep of Walker Bay, and it is here that aficionados come from afar to study and enjoy the whales.

Indeed, Walker Bay is recognized by the World Wide Fund for Nature (WWF) as one of the world's twelve premier whale-viewing locations. From vantage points on the cliffs and rocks of the area one can clearly see the animals and view them at leisure – sometimes from as close as ten metres.

Southern rights – the numbers range from 60 to 100 and more – usually begin to appear in Walker Bay in June and can be seen until November. Calving peaks during July and August, the viewing season extending through September and October. Daily sightings are pretty well guaranteed during this period; 20 and more whales can often be observed in the waters at one time.

Hermanus, popular among holiday-makers and the more affluent of retired people, is a sprawling, fairly substantial town attractively set between mountain and sea. The place once served as the bustling centre of the fishing industry and it has a charming

TOP: Leisure craft at anchor in Gordon's Bay. ABOVE: Whale-spotting in comfort from the cliffs above Hermanus.

The cliff-girded waters of Walker Bay, one of the world's premier whale-watching venues. Most of the bayshore falls within the Walker Bay Nature Reserve.

old harbour. The quayside no longer echoes the sirens of the incoming boats and the cries of the mongers, but there's another harbour next door, a fine new one that hosts both bobbing leisure craft and work-worn trawlers. Some of the smaller vessels can be hired for deep-sea tunny and marlin expeditions.

Much of the bayshore and its immediate hinterland – almost the entire coastal strip from Hermanus through to Die Kelders (see opposite page) – has been set aside as the Walker Bay Nature Reserve.

There are a number of rewarding walks behind and to either side of the town; especially recommended for whale-watchers is the 12-kilometre route along the top of the cliffs, from the New Harbour east to Klein River Lagoon, along which there are lovely views of the rocky shoreline and its coves. Even grander are the vistas that unfold along the Rotary Mountain Way, a scenic drive that cuts through the backing Kleinrivier hills, heights that rise abruptly from nearly 60 to 900 metres above sea level.

One excellent elevated vantage point is Dreunkrans, which you reach by driving south along Westcliff Road. Park in Marine Drive or at Fick's Pool, and take the cliff path towards the New Harbour. Also inviting are the terraces above the Old Harbour, where there's a telescope, and a plaque giving basic information about Walker Bay and its whales. Among other strategic spots:
◆ A good place to start is Gearing's Point (a gravelled area next to the Old Harbour), which affords a splendid view of the entire bay.
◆ Windsor Bay (park on Marine Drive), where whales can be observed from the comfort of your car.
◆ Die Gang: drive northeast along Main Road towards the beaches; turn off just after the pedestrian crossing at Berg-en-See.
◆ Kwaaiwater: viewing spots accessible by car.
◆ The Voëlklip and Grotto beaches. Here, the southern rights are sometimes observed breaching; bathers have occasionally come into close and uncomfortable contact with a surfacing whale.
Among the more spectacular of dolphin sightings occur when there are sardine (pilchard) runs in the bay, pinpointed by the 'ribbons' of Cape cormorants that follow large schools of the common species. One or two Bryde's whales usually follow the procession. Small groups of bottlenose dolphins also make their sporadic appearance, coming quite close inshore.

Whale-watching boat safaris were a popular feature during the early 1990s, but these threatened to harm Walker Bay's reputation as a prime land-based whale-watching site (and perhaps the animals themselves), and the practice ceased following a public outcry. The laws were recently relaxed to allow closer boat-based observation along South Africa's coasts but certain areas – including Walker Bay – remain no-go zones.

The annual Whale Festival, an 11-day extravaganza of music, theatre, art shows, sports, crafts and flower exhibitions and much else, is held during September. Construction of the Whale House – a museum complex of display and lecture rooms on Market Square – is almost complete.

GANSBAAI TO AGULHAS

The entire coastline from Die Kelders, on Walker Bay's eastern shore, to Pearly Beach offers excellent whale-watching opportunities. Especially well placed for viewing are the limestone cliffs at Die Kelders, a sequence of caves through which an underground stream flows.

A couple of kilometres to the south is Gansbaai, a fairly substantial village where you can buy fresh fish on the quayside and walk along the breakwater. From here there are splendid views of the blue ocean and, some way to the southwest, notorious Danger

HARK THE HERALD
Hermanus is the only town in the world that employs a whale crier, a herald who patrols the streets blowing his kelp-horn to alert passers-by to the presence, and whereabouts, of the whales which swim in close to the steep cliffs which border the town. The sounds are in a kind of Morse code, the sequence identifying the different venues. Translations appear on the sandwich board the crier carries.

Reports of sightings are also recorded by the Hermanus Tourism Bureau in Main Road. Phone them on (0283) 2 2629, or dial the toll-free Whale Hotline, 083 910 1028.

Point (see box). The long stretch of coast running away to the east is especially rugged, undeveloped for the most part, and until recently one had to loop inland to reach the few tiny seaside settlements, among them Franskraal, Kleinbaai, Uilenkraalsmond and Pearly Beach (there is now a tarred connecting road). One of these loops takes you to Elim, a picturesque little village of beautifully thatched cottages which has changed hardly at all since it was founded, as a Moravian mission station, in 1824. Its German-made church clock, which first started ticking in 1764, still keeps good time.

Southernmost point along this coastal stretch, indeed the southern extremity of the African continent, is Cape Agulhas, the name derived from the Portuguese word for 'needles'. This is probably not a reference to the physical nature of the area but to its position on the map: here, the early navigators found that their ships' compasses were not affected by magnetic deviation but bore 'directly upon the true poles of the earth'.

Otherwise, Agulhas holds little of interest. The Cape itself is the southern segment of an inland plain which slips quietly beneath the sea to become the vast (250-km wide), shallow Agulhas Bank, the most extensive part of southern Africa's continental shelf and among the world's richest fishing grounds.

The Agulhas lighthouse is the country's second oldest, built in the style of the great Pharos tower at Alexandra, in ancient Egypt, and a lifesaving friend to sailors since 1848. Inside is a museum (the only one of its kind in southern Africa) that tells the story of lighthouses generally and this one in particular. It forms part of the Bredasdorp Shipwreck museum complex (see box).

Beyond Agulhas, to the east, are Struisbaai, which boasts a small harbour and a superb expanse of beach (good whale-viewing), and the De Mond Nature Reserve, a peaceful and wholly unspoilt place of milkwood trees, mountain cypresses, kloofs, rock pools and a river estuary that attracts a wealth of birds (including the martial eagle and the rare Knysna woodpecker).

Bredasdorp, some 25 km inland from Agulhas, is the area's principal town and centre of a pleasant and prosperous agricultural district (wool, grain, dairy products). Well worth visiting is the local mountain reserve, famed for its wild flowers, among them giant proteas, ericas and the brilliant Bredasdorp lily.

ARNISTON TO DE HOOP

The enchanting little fishing village of Arniston, set on the shores of Marcus Bay, takes its English name from an especially tragic shipwreck. It is also known by the Afrikaans name Waenhuiskrans, which refers to the enormous sea cave carved out of the nearby cliffs, a cavern so large that it seemed, to the early settlers, quite wide and tall enough to serve as a coach house ('waenhuis') able to host several wagons and their spans of oxen. Also of interest along this stretch of coast are the giant pods of the *Entada gigas* sea-bean, and the fish traps built and used by the prehistoric Strandloper ('beach-ranger') people who were seasonal residents of the area.

Arniston itself is known for its lovely little thatched cottages, for the raucous and amiable fishermen who hawk their catches at the harbour, and for its fine hotel, one of the gems of the South African hospitality industry. Walks along the shore to the west yield excellent whale-watching opportunities.

The magnificent De Hoop Nature Reserve, along the coast from Arniston, is one of the country's most important sanctuaries: it sprawls across some 36 000 hectares of lowland and coastal fynbos (the largest remaining expanse of this indigenous Cape vegetation) and is home to a full 1 500 different plant species – 50 of which are unique to this particular area and 70 of which are classed as endangered or rare. The area embraces great, rolling sand dunes, limestone hills, an extensive vlei (marsh), a section of the Potberg mountain range, and a splendid number and variety of birds.

The adjacent marine reserve extends 5 kilometres out to sea and, in the spring and summer months, hosts the biggest concentration of southern right cow-calf pairs. Altogether, 13 types of marine mammal visit these waters, and although one's encounters with them are not as close as those in Walker Bay (see page 32), sheer numbers, combined with the superb scenery and the myriad and fascinating life forms of the tidal pools, create an experience that will long remain in the memory.

Next door St Sebastian Bay is also noted for its visiting whales. Southernmost point here is Cape Infanta, overlooking the Breede River mouth and, across the broad estuary, the popular little resort of Witsand. The area, part of the Garden Route (see next chapter), is a mecca for anglers, and for those partial to oysters and other shellfish.

Fun on the beach at Arniston, one of the Overberg's most appealing coastal villages. The shoreline to the west offers splendid whale-watching opportunities.

The Garden Route

The evening sun bathes the enchanting Tsitsikamma seaboard in its soft light. The offshore waters are a proclaimed marine reserve.

*T*his part of the southern coastal belt extends from the inland town of Heidelberg and the pretty little seaside village of Witsand (see also page 37) east to the green and pleasant Tsitsikamma National Park – a 300-km stretch of coast and countryside renowned for its scenic beauty.

To the north are the slopes of the Outeniqua and Tsitsikamma mountains, blessed by good year-round rains and highland streams that, together, nurture the region's dense forests. Here are deep valleys, spectacular mountain passes, waterfalls, secluded and secret ravines clothed in thick, moist mantles of greenery. To the south are the warm blue waters of the Indian Ocean and in the middle lies the coastal terrace, the famed 'garden' which so entranced Francois le Vaillant, the noted 18th-century French traveller. 'Nature', he wrote, 'has made an enchanted abode of this beautiful place.'

Predictably, the Garden Route has become a prime holiday, second-home and retirement venue and much of the seaboard has been taken over by developers. But the essence of the region – a countryside that both delights the eye and refreshes the spirit – remains unchanged. And the whales still come inshore to mate and calve.

STILBAAI TO MOSSEL BAY

Known as the 'Bay of the Sleeping Beauty', Stilbaai is a pleasant little resort town that boasts a busy fishing harbour and a surrounding countryside graced by a superb indigenous (fynbos) plant life. The wild flowers put on their best faces between July and

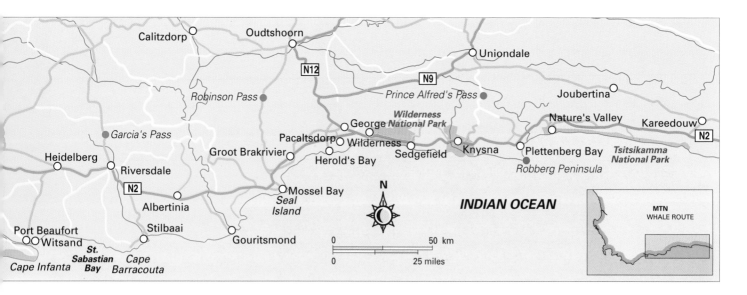

October. The immediate area, in fact, supports three nature reserves and three botanical gardens, one of which has been established in a previously marginalised ('black') township to serve as a model for other urban centres.

Stilbaai tends to be crowded with holiday-makers in summer (it's especially popular among farming folk); they come for, among other things, its wide beach, safe sea-bathing, and for the good fishing to be had in both the ocean (rock, surf, deep-sea) and estuary. The river is navigable for 14 km, and its eels are famous: many weigh an impressive 7 kg and more and, curiously, they are quite tame (a quality reinforced at 11.00 each morning, when they are fed at a spot called Palinggat).

There's plenty, too, for the whale-watcher: scores of the animals come into the bay between June and October. Among prime viewing sites are the panoramic whale lookout above the harbour; the dunes overlooking Preekstoel; Lappiesbaai – and Tapaz deck; the lookout in the attractive Pauline Bohnen reserve, and most of the parking areas in Jongensfontein.

To the east, in the Gouritzmond area, is Rein's Nature Reserve, a treasure house of fynbos (heath-type) plants and a fine place for whale-watching. Farther along the coast lies Mossel Bay, named for the fine mussels that provided food for the ancient Khoikhoi 'Strandloper' folk who were seasonal residents of the area. The bay was also known to the earliest European seafarers: Bartholomeu Dias, Vasco da Gama and other navigators filled their water caskets from the perennial spring. In 1501 the Portuguese admiral Jão da Nova erected a small stone chapel, the country's first European style building (nothing remains of this edifice). Some while later a ship's captain placed his report in the hollow trunk of a large milkwood tree, for collection by the next fleet that passed by; other mariners also used the tree for mail delivery, so establishing the country's first 'post office'. The tree, now a venerably gnarled specimen, has survived the centuries and is part of the town's impressive Bartholomeu Dias Museum, which embraces much else relating to the exploration and colonization of the region.

Mossel Bay is a fairly large town, focal point of the drive to exploit South Africa's offshore oil reserves and, more traditionally, a holiday and recreational area popular for its beaches. The place, according to the Guinness Book of Records, is second only to Hawaii in the all-year mildness of its climate.

Southern rights are common in the local waters during the season; humpbacks are often seen between May and December; killer whales are occasionally spotted. Bryde's whales, which don't often come inshore, are year-round visitors. The best viewing sites are at the Point; in the area adjoining the Tourism Bureau, and at De Bakke and Santos beaches. Recommended spots in the wider area include the Vleesbaai beach and caravan park; Dana Bay's First and Second beaches, the beach at Hartenbos (a busy seaside and river resort) and the coast around Klein Brakrivier (Little Brak River).

And there's plenty of other marine life to see and enjoy. Huge schools of common dolphins, numbering in their hundreds if not thousands, can sometimes be seen in the bay and along the St Blaize hiking trail; the bottlenose species is also a familiar sight.

Seal Island, within the bay, is home to around 12 000 of these marine mammals and may be visited (cruises start from Mossel Bay harbour). Among the area's many seabird species are the jackass penguin, the kelp gull, the endangered black oystercatcher and the Cape gannet.

TOP: *Yachts moored in Mossel Bay harbour.* CENTRE: *Humpback whales migrate along the Garden Route's coast during June and July.* ABOVE: *The 'Outeniqua Choo-tjoe', a vintage steam train, chugs across the Kaaimans River on its way to Knysna.*

WATCH FOR...

◆ Southern right whales: anywhere along this coast.

◆ Bryde's and, to a lesser degree, minke whales in autumn and early winter; often seen, together with frenzied dolphins and gannets, following the fish shoals.

◆ Humpback whales, most notably in June and July and especially off the Knysna Heads and Plettenberg Bay.

◆ Occasional killer whales.

◆ Sperm whales, though oceanic animals, are sometimes glimpsed out to sea.

◆ Dolphin visitors include the bottlenose, the common and, notably in the Plettenberg Bay area, the humpback.

◆ Cape fur seals (below): anywhere, but especially on Mossel Bay's Seal Island, which supports a 12 000-strong colony, and around Plettenberg Bay. The southern elephant seal is a frequent vagrant. Plettenberg Bay is arguably the finest all-round viewing area for marine mammals.

For information, call the MTN Whale Hotline on 083 910 1028.

The Wilderness coastline is fringed by broad, gently shelving sands; the area's renowned lakes lie a little way inland.

GEORGE AND WILDERNESS

Set at the foot of the grand Outeniqua mountains a short distance inland, George (named, in 1811, after England's King George the Third) is an attractive town of broad, oak-lined streets and ranks as the Garden Route's principal centre. Well worth visiting is the Drostdy Museum (the building dates from 1812; among displays is a splendid collection of old musical instruments), St Mark's Cathedral, and St Peter's and St Paul's, the country's oldest Roman Catholic church.

Along the coast to the south are a number of prime whale-spotting venues, among them Herold's Bay, a resort set in a sheltered cove; Glentana and, 15 km to the east, pretty little Victoria Bay (also a prime surfing area). The latter is well served by guest-houses; notable is that at The Point: claimed to be closer to the sea than any other in Africa, it has a special terrace for whale-viewing.

The national highway (N2) links George with the region's main centres, but there are other and perhaps more inviting routes, certainly in the initial stages. The Old Passes Road, for instance, loops inland through an entrancing countryside of fern forest and woodland to reach Knysna. There's also the famed 'Outeniqua Choo-tjoe', a vintage Class 24 narrow-guage steam train that will take you on a slow, comfortable and entirely memorable journey along one of the world's most beautiful seaboards.

A dozen kilometres or so southeast of George is Wilderness, a charming, rather spread-out seaside resort centre and focal point of South Africa's 'Lake District'. The town nestles around a lagoon (in reality, the mouth of the Touws River) that forms the first link in a chain of coastal lakes stretching almost as far as Knysna, 40 km distant. There are six others, by name Swartvlei, Rondevlei, Langvlei, Groenvlei and, rather smaller, the Serpentine and Island Lake (Eilandvlei), and they are magical expanses of water, four of them embraced within the Wilderness National Park (this sanctuary also encompasses five rivers, two estuaries and 28 km of coastline).

The area, whose natural assets are managed and its development monitored by the National Parks Board, has excellent tourism facilities. Swartvlei and Island Lake are much favoured by watersports enthusiasts, the entire region by hikers, ramblers, bird-watchers and nature-lovers. Dolphin's Point (on the main road) is perhaps the best of the whale-watching viewsites.

At the eastern end of the lakes area is Sedgefield, a tranquil village that hugs Swartvlei's shores and which is reached via the N2. A longer but arguably more attractive drive, though, is the gravel road that meanders past the lakes. Close by is the Goukamma Nature Reserve, a 2 230-hectare sanctuary which takes in Groenvlei, the lower reaches of the Goukamma River, its estuary and the rocks, dunes, magnificent beaches and the offshore waters (this is the marine reserve section) along 14 km of enchantingly pristine coastline.

There's good whale-viewing near Sedgefield itself, at Swartvlei mouth and beach, Gericke's Point and Myoli Beach; in the Goukamma reserve at Buffels Bay (look for the MTN interpretative board) and at Platbank, a high vantage point behind the Lake Pleasant Hotel.

THE KNYSNA AREA

Knysna's motto – 'This fair land, the gift of God' – pays fitting tribute to the beauty of the densely forested countryside, the superb coastline and, most especially, to one of the country's largest and most attractive tidal lagoons. The latter, a 17-km long stretch of tranquil, reflective water, is fed by both river and sea, which enters through a narrow inlet guarded by two high sandstone cliffs known as The Heads.

There are superb views of the tree-girded town, lagoon, Leisure Island (an upmarket residential area) and the sea from the eastern Head; the western one accommodates the Featherbed Bay private nature reserve, which is open to the public, accessible by boat and worth a visit for its guided nature trails and gourmet restaurant.

The lagoon is popular among holiday-makers of both the active and the contemplative kind, its waters ideal for angling, canoeing, cruising (craft are available for hire), water-skiing and for just messing about in boats, its banks for walking and bird-watching in the loveliest of surrounds. The lagoon is also a treasure house of life forms, renowned for the number and variety of its fish, crabs, prawns, oysters (these find their way to the most discriminating tables in southern Africa and farther afield) and for the rare seahorse *Hippocampus capensis*, which is found nowhere else.

Special, too, is the Knysna Forest which, when combined with that of the adjacent Tsitsikamma area, forms the country's largest expanse of indigenous montane forest

BELOW: The charming little village of Sedgefield hugs the shores of Swartvlei, among the largest of the region's lakes. BOTTOM: Knysna Lagoon plays host to a myriad small boats.

WHEN IN KNYSNA ...

Knysna is noted for its honey, cheese, ham, trout, oysters (see text), and furniture made from the local hardwoods; its rich and tasty draught ale (Mitchell's Brewery welcomes visitors); and its coffee shops, boutiques and galleries. Among specific features of interest:

◆ Millwood House (below), built in 1886 at the early gold diggings 25 km away, in the Gouveld forest, and later re-erected piece by piece in town to serve as a museum. Displays include relics of the gold rush. Next-door Parkes Cottage (also transplanted) and Parkes Shop focus on the timber industry.

◆ The station, terminus of the 'Outeniqua Choo-tjoe' steam railway.
◆ The Old Gaol Complex, which embraces the Angling Museum, the Maritime Museum, the Knysna Art Gallery, the atmospheric Old Gaol Café and a gift shop. The complex is on the site of the original gaol, first building to be erected in Knysna; its inmates helped build the scenic (and at the time immensely important) Prince Alfred's Pass through the spectacular backing mountains.
◆ The oyster-tasting tavern (run by the Knysna Oyster Company) on Thesen Island.
◆ For shopping, try Woodmill Lane (Main and Long streets, and site of an early sawmill), a busy complex of craft shops, pubs, open-air restaurants; and the Knysna Quays, on the waterfront, which offers similar enticements.

Plettenberg Bay's Beacon Island and its modern hotel-timeshare complex.

(36 000 hectares). Trails through its dark-green depths lead past stately ironwood and stinkwood, kamassie (Knysna boxwood), white alder, blackwood and, most specially, massive and ancient yellowwood trees.

The most rewarding of the the area's whale-spotting venues are The Heads, where there are MTN interpretative boards; at Brenton-on-Sea, a pretty little resort village just to the west (the local church is worth a visit); and just beyond at Buffels Bay. There are quite lovely walks, and fine whale-watching, in the Brenton area, most especially the 3-km hike (known as Fisherman's Walk) along the top of Brenton Cliffs. This is also a prime viewing area for dolphins which surf the waves that roll into the secluded little coves.

PLETTENBERG BAY TO TSITSIKAMMA

There can be few places on earth blessed with a better climate and more beautiful surrounds than Plettenberg Bay: it enjoys a full 320 days of uninterrupted sunshine a year, a kind of eternal springtime that brings bright clarity to the area's three superb beaches and a hinterland of hill, forest, rivers, wetlands and great swathes of unspoilt Cape flora. The town itself is small, attractive, bustling, and it has all the amenities.

The bay's most prominent landmark is Beacon Island (connected to the shore by a causeway), which supports an impressive hotel and time-share complex. To the southwest a high red-sandstone headland probes 4 km into the warm waters of the Indian Ocean, sheltering the beaches from prevailing wind. The distinctive promontory ends at a point named Cape Seal; its northern shore is lined by almost sheer cliffs; the southern slopes are less dramatic, and the whole of the peninsula has been proclaimed as the Robberg ('seal mountain') Nature Reserve.

Robberg is noted for its bird life (white-breasted cormorants, black oystercatchers and southern black-backed gulls breed in the area); for the marine life of the intertidal zone, and for caves that once sheltered early Khoikhoi communities.

Two other areas beckon the nature-lover. A few kilometres to the northeast are the Keurbooms River and the adjoining Whiskey Creek reserves. And farther east is Nature's Valley, a small village and reserve in a superb setting of mountain, forest, lagoon and sea.

Some 80 km of the coastal strip running east from Nature's Valley, together with 5 km of the fringing ocean, has been set aside as the Tsitsikamma National Park – one of the country's most beautiful. The land area, cut through by numerous little rivers and streams, is endowed with a rich plant life and some 280 bird species.

The rock pools of the shoreline teem with life, as does the sea itself. Within the marine park (the first of its kind in Africa) there are underwater trails for swimmers, snorklers and scuba divers.

Whales and dolphins are often seen sporting beyond the breakers. Indeed, there's good whale- and dolphin-watching along the entire section of coast from Plettenberg Bay to Storms River. The cliffs that line the rugged Tsitsikamma shore – some rise 200 metres above the sea – provide excellent vantage points, as does Nature's Valley. Those in and around Plettenberg Bay include: Lookout Beach (ice-cold beer while you wait); Signal Hill (drive towards Central Beach and take Sinclair Street to your right); the Robberg Nature Reserve (there's a seal colony on the eastern side, and dolphins are a familiar sight); Kranshoek (on the Knysna side of the bay); the rocks of Beacon Island; Keurbooms Strand, and Robberg Beach.

The tranquil Keurbooms River resort, set within a nature reserve.

THE OTTER TRAIL

The first of the country's organized trails to be established and still a favourite among hikers, the Otter Trail winds its way through the Tsitsikamma National Park.

The five-day, 41-km route leads from Storms River Mouth to Nature's Valley in the west (picture above shows the Valley's river estuary), taking hikers through a superb countryside of dense natural forest, fast-flowing streams, waterfalls, cliffs, rocks, tidal pools and beaches. The trail follows the coastline for most of the way; the longest daily stretch is 14 km, and there is plenty of time to stop, study the flora, the bird and marine life, snorkel, swim, sunbathe, enjoy the vistas – and watch for the coming of the whales. Overnight accommodation is provided in simple cabins. Bookings through the National Parks Board (see page 102).

The Eastern Seaboard

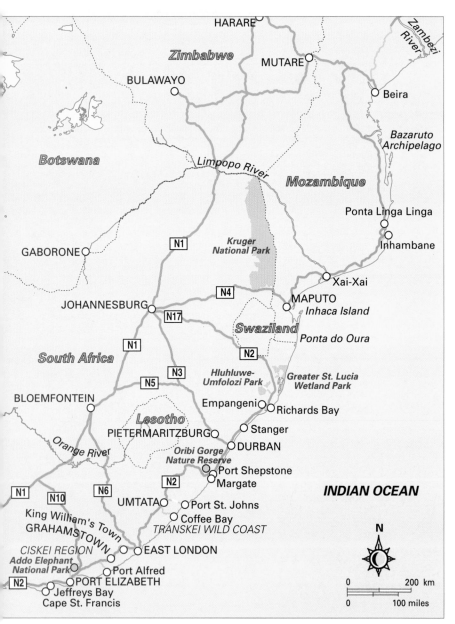

The coasts that run around the eastern flank of southern Africa, from Port Elizabeth to the mouth of the Zambezi River in Mozambique, are washed by the Indian Ocean – and they're quite different in character from those in the west (pages 17-26). Here there is no Antarctic stream to chill the waters, no arid sandveld but, rather, the warmth and lushness conferred (largely) by the southward flowing, Indo-tropic Mozambique-Agulhas current. The climate is wetter, the earth more generous, the coastal belt far more developed and heavily populated – and more popular among holiday-makers.

The first and by far the longest stretch, to a point just south of Richards Bay in northern KwaZulu-Natal, is fairly straight, its most notable irregularity Durban's 8-km long Bluff. The shoreline, though, is anything but featureless. On the contrary, the sandy beaches, often backed by dunes and flanked by tumbles of rocks; the vegetation, which becomes more tropically luxurious the farther north one travels; the scenic beauty of the immediate hinterland and the warm and equable climate, all combine to create one of the southern hemisphere's most attractive seaboards.

The second, shorter, stretch is the northern coastal zone, which is part of the extensive Mozambique coastal plain. Here the vegetated dunes just behind the shoreline are among the highest in the world, but the general region is flat, sandy and bushy, the climate very hot and humid.

THE EASTERN CAPE

Port Elizabeth, the country's fifth city and third largest seaport, is set on the shores of Algoa Bay, an attractive metropolis known for its status as headquarters of South Africa's motor industry; its busy harbour; its English colonial-style architecture; its fine, open beaches (there are four of them), and its oceanarium.

The latter, part of a multi-faceted museum complex (it holds the world's third largest collection of marine mammal specimens), ranks among Africa's foremost marine research centres. It is also a prime tourist attraction, popular for the bottlenose dolphins that show off their intelligence and acrobatic skills as part of an ongoing effort to promote awareness of our precious natural heritage and the need to conserve it. Cape fur seals also get into the act.

To the west of Port Elizabeth is St Francis Bay, a broad sweep of coastline distinguished by its splendid sands and resort centres. Most notable of these is Jeffrey's Bay, famed for its great surfing rollers and for the lovely seashells found along its shores. Rather less heavily developed is the maritime belt to the east of Port Elizabeth – the shores of Algoa Bay, followed by the stretch to the Great Fish River. Beyond lies the Ciskei region, whose seaboard offers lovely expanses of golden, gently sloping sand.

Between Ciskei and its twin, the Transkei region, is East London, a pleasant little seaside city and the country's only major river port. The harbour fills the mouth of the Buffalo River, which rises in the high and beautiful Amatola mountains to the north-west. Well worth visiting is its museum, repository for the first coelocanth to be caught in modern times (this immensely primitive fish lived some 250 million years ago, and was thought to have been long extinct); for its fine display of Karoo fossils, and for the world's only surviving dodo's egg. The city's aquarium, on the Esplanade, is smallish but its 400-plus marine species are well chosen; also in residence are penguins, seals (seal shows are held twice a day) and a number of oil-polluted and otherwise injured sea creatures that are being nurtured back to health.

Transkei's seaboard, which runs northwestwards from the Great Kei to the Mtamvuna River, is known as the Wild Coast – an evocative name for an enchanting maritime wilderness of sandy bays, rugged cliffs and rocky reefs, of river estuaries, lush green hills and deep-green woodlands. Fully 18 rivers find their way, many of them in remarkably convoluted fashion, through the hinterland to the ocean; the largest coastal centres are Coffee Bay and Port St Johns; the most prominent physical feature the Hole-in-the-Wall, a massive detached cliff with an arched opening through which the surf thunders. Near the northern end of the stretch is the Wild Coast Sun hotel, casino and resort complex.

KWAZULU-NATAL

Durban is distinguished by what is arguably the southern hemisphere's finest natural harbour, an almost entirely enclosed expanse of water so splendidly spacious that Vasco da Gama, the first Portuguese navigator who passed this way – at Christmastime in 1497 – believed it was a lagoon at the mouth of a major river, and called it Rio de Natal ('River of the Nativity').

Today the city functions as the country's largest seaport and among the most popular of its holiday destinations, known for, among much else, the magnificent ocean rollers and broad white beaches that gird the city's Golden Mile. Special features of interest along this 6-km, highly commercialized strip are the Fitzsimon's Snake Park, which houses all manner of reptiles of both local and exotic origin; and Sea World, renowned for its dolphinarium and aquarium. Here, as in Port Elizabeth, Cape fur seals

Top: A seal plays to the gallery in Port Elizabeth's splendid oceanarium. Centre: A bottlenose 'porpoises' in Algoa Bay. Above: A humpback whale breaching in spectacular style.

VIEWING VENUES

◆ The stretch from Cape St Francis to the Transkei offers a myriad vantage points; humpback, Bryde's, minke and killer whales and humpback dolphins come quite close inshore; southern rights (up to 20 a day in Algoa Bay); also large pods of bottlenose and common dolphins (a spectacular sight in the surf breakers), the latter sometimes numbering in their thousands as they feed frantically, in company with gannets and a whale or two, on the winter fish runs.

Transkei also offers especially good viewing – the continental shelf here is narrow, which means there's deep water close inshore – but some of the best vantage points are difficult to get to. Sperm and beaked whales approach especially close off the coast at Port St Johns.

◆ Port St Johns to KwaZulu-Natal: a few southern rights in season; occasional humpback whales, notably off Cape Vidal. Huge shoals of common dolphins follow the annual 'sardine run' (July-August). Also bottlenose and humpback dolphins, though the latter are declining (probably due to shark nets and coastal degradation). Spotted dolphins can sometimes be seen.

◆ Mozambique: vantage points are few and often difficult to access. Bottlenose and humpback dolphins fairly common between Ponto do Ouro and Maputo. There's nothing much in Maputo Bay but nearby Inhaca Island yields large numbers of bottlenoses and the occasional dugong. The latter, a grievously persecuted animal, is at its most plentiful in Inhambane Bay and around the Bazaruto islands. The stretch between Maputo and Beira is flat, but humpback whales can be seen quite close to the coast; minkes enter bays and lagoons; dolphins (humpback, bottlenose, spotted and spinner) are abundant enough.

Trek fishermen haul their day's catch onto Durban's Addington beach. Among the beachfront's major attractions is Sea World and its dolphinarium.

and penguins join the dolphins in putting on delightful public performances; the sharks are fed three times a week.

The seaboard that runs south from Durban is one of Africa's most enticing, numbering among its assets a balmy subtropical climate, the warm and welcoming waters of the Indian Ocean, splendid stretches of sand, river estuaries and lagoons, a green and pleasant hinterland and a multitude of pretty little seaside towns and villages. Rather quieter but no less attractive are the coasts to the north of Durban.

The far northern reaches of KwaZulu-Natal – the territory bounded by the Lebombo mountains and Mozambique – is known as Maputaland, a region of stunning diversity: this is the transitional zone between the tropics and subtropics, and within its bounds are half a dozen different, major ecosystems. The visual variety is perhaps at its most evident along the coast: flanking the shores are three large lake systems, biggest of them St Lucia – an extensive and environmentally unique wetland complex of shallow lagoon and estuary, lily-covered pan, grassland, forest, high dune and marine sanctuary. Inland are several game areas that rank among Africa's finest (including the famed Hluhluwe-Umfolozi, Mkuzi, and Ndumo parks); farther up the shoreline lie Lake Sibaya, South Africa's largest stretch of fresh water, and the Kosi Bay Nature Reserve, a wonderland of mangrove, limpid lake and dune.

The beaches along this northern strip serve as the breeding ground of giant and once-endangered leatherback and loggerhead turtles. Offshore are the world's most southerly and, for the scuba-diver and snorkler, some of its most rewarding coral reefs.

MOZAMBIQUE

Maputo, the country's capital, lies near the southern extremity of a 2 500-km coastline that extends to the Rovumo River, which forms the border with Tanzania. Technically, though, the northern limit of the southern African region is the Zambezi River, which discharges into the Indian Ocean near Beira.

The entire maritime belt is low-lying country, its highest points barely 250 m above sea level. Strong inshore currents, running counter to the tropical Mozambique stream, have created a medley of sandbars, dune-backed lagoons and small offshore islands; the beaches are coral-fringed, broad and, most of them, quite deserted.

Maputo itself, though, has come alive since the civil war ended: foreign enterprises have moved in, and the holiday-makers – notably South Africans – are coming back in increasing numbers; hotels, restaurants, bars and nightspots are proliferating. In the Gulf of Maputo, 35 km from the city, is Inhaca Island, fringed by mangroves in the north, bright coral reefs in the west and famed for the clarity of the surrounding sea. There is a ferry service to, and hotel accommodation on, the island.

Farther north are the twin towns of Inhambane and Maxixe, the former founded by the Portuguese in 1534 although the area hosted foreigners – Arab and Persian traders – as early as the 10th century. It still has a discernably exotic atmosphere; worth visiting is the 200-year old cathedral.

The seaside town of Vilankulo, some 700 km from Maputo, is a fairly substantial centre notable for its proximity to a group of islands known as the Bazaruto Archipelago and now a national park. Between them, the three main ones sustain 180 species of bird, crocodile, suni antelope and some lovely butterflies. It is the sea and its beaches, though, that attract visitors: the reefs, enveloped by the clearest of blue water (the blue ranges from very dark to very pale), are a paradise for divers. In the depths are dolphin and dugong, giant lobsters, several kinds of marine turtle and a splendid array of game fish.

Finally, there's Beira, Mozambique's second city and a major port located at the sandy mouth of the Pungoe River. It has most of the amenities appropriate to its status, but access can be difficult: the coast road has been upgraded but can be problematic. The best route in is the 600-km highway from Mutare in Zimbabwe, though a more rewarding way of getting there is by ship (expensive) or private boat. Indeed, road travel throughout the country is a bit of a challenge (don't drive at night); the coastal centres are poorly linked and to travel from one to another it is often easier either to embark on a long inland detour or take passage on a dhow.

BELOW: A white rhino in the Hluhluwe-Umfolozi Park. CENTRE: Giant logger-head turtles breed along the east coast; this female is digging a nest, with her flippers, preparatory to laying her many eggs. BOTTOM: Benguerra Island, in the Indian Ocean off Mozambique.

SOUTHERN AFRICAN MARINE MAMMALS:

Species Profiles

The focus in the following pages is on the whales, dolphins and seals that occur in southern African waters. Some, like the southern right, humpback and Bryde's whales, the bottlenose, common and humpback dolphins and the Cape fur seal, are either resident in or regular visitors to the region; others appear sporadically; still others only occasionally, as vagrants. This is the page order in which they are profiled.

Southern Right Whale

Eubalaena australis

TYPE: Baleen whale (Family Balaenidae)
MAXIMUM LENGTH: 15 to 17 m
MAXIMUM WEIGHT:
50 to 65 t when full grown
CONSERVATION STATUS: Vulnerable; the population is recovering, but the level of recovery is still not high enough to ensure that the species is out of danger.

Description

The southern right whale does not have a dorsal fin. It is also characterized by highly arched jaws, with long (up to 2.5 m), dark baleen. It also has a number of whitish, wart-like protuberances on its head. Generally, these are large, dark whales with a characteristic V-shaped blow. Their colour is mostly black, though some may have white blotches and appear mottled. Calves (in particular) may be completely white.

The species is a large, robust and rotund animal that normally appears in winter. During other periods, however – especially from August to October – it can be seen in pairs or small groups performing aerial displays, which may possibly be associated with courtship. These include leaping almost clear of the water (known as breaching) and beating the water surface with the tail (lobtailing). If you see a large, dark tail-fluke held aloft for several minutes, almost as if the whale were standing on its head, then you have definitely seen a southern right whale. This is known as 'sailing', and can often be seen in protected bays.

BELOW: A southern right breaks the surface. BELOW RIGHT: The flipper is held aloft in a typical pose.

Right whales breach in spectacular fashion, thrusting their bodies almost clear of the water.

Where and when to view

Between about June and November, these animals can best be observed from promontories bordering large bays, throughout the southern and southeastern Cape coastal region. A few even find their way as far north as southern KwaZulu-Natal.

Biology

Southern right whales are very similar to the right whales of the northern hemisphere – hence the two related names. The southern species occurs in all the southern seas and, in autumn, migrates northwards to sheltered coastal bays as far north as the tropics. Here they not only avoid the coldness of the southern seas, but also give birth to young and, apparently, also mate. A single calf is born after a gestation period of 11 to 12 months. The newborn calf is large – 5 to 6 m in length – but remains very dependent on the mother, from whom it suckles for at least six months. In spring, when the calves are a few months old, the whales make their way slowly southwards to the sub-Antarctic convergence (55 °S), where they spend the summer months.

Southern right whales apparently do not feed while in our waters, although plankton and small crustaceans have been found in the stomachs of animals stranded on beaches. For the mother to suckle a 5-m calf while not feeding herself must drain a great deal of her energy.

Recent research shows that the whales visit the region's waters on a three-year cycle. This, and much of the other information we have, has been gathered by monitoring strandings and from an annual photographic survey along the South African coast, where as many animals as possible are identified. The identifications are compared with photographic material from previous years.

Apart from the pygmy right whale, the other baleen whales likely to be seen off the southern and southeastern coasts are all rorquals (Family Balaenopteridae) and, unlike southern right whales, all have dorsal fins. These whales are more slender than southern rights, and their mouths are not so distinctly arched. Rorquals also have 'grooved' throats, which enables them to take in copious amounts of water when feeding.

Pygmy Right Whale

Caperea marginata

TYPE: Baleen whale (Family Neobalaenidae)
MAXIMUM LENGTH: 6.5 m
MAXIMUM WEIGHT: 3.2 t
CONSERVATION STATUS: Insufficiently known; considered rare. There is no information on the size of the population.

Description

This is the smallest of the baleen whales. Adult females are slightly bigger than adult males (about 6.3 m and 6 m respectively). The species is more slender than the right whale, and has a small, triangular, hooked dorsal fin two-thirds of a body-length from the snout. The jaws are strongly arched, the flippers small and tapered to a rounded tip. The top of the head, body, flukes, upper half and tip of the lower jaws and the outer surface of the flipper are dark grey or black. In contrast, the belly, underside of the flipper and flukes are pale grey or whitish. The lips of the upper jaw are white, and the baleen plates ivory-colored with a dark outer margin. Young whales are lighter in colour than adults. Pygmy right whales resemble minke whales in silhouette, which often causes confusion.

Where and when to view

Pygmy right whales are restricted to the waters of the southern hemisphere, with a circumpolar distribution from the Antarctic Convergence to about Latitude 32 °S. However, with fewer than 100 or so records in existence, the chances of seeing one of these whales is extremely small.

Biology

The scarcity of records – both strandings and sightings – means that almost nothing is known of the biology and behaviour of this whale. Nevertheless, the few free-ranging animals observed have yielded some behavioural information. When seen inshore, they show a strong preference for sheltered embayments such as False Bay, Mossel Bay, Plettenberg Bay and Algoa Bay. Unlike

right whales, they do not appear to breach or display their flukes and flippers, and even the dorsal fin is seldom seen above the surface. They swim at up to 8 km/h and seem to be shallow divers, spending less than five minutes submerged. The blow is small and inconspicuous. This, coupled with the small size of the whale and its similarity to minke whales, make sightings and identification difficult and probably accounts for the species' apparent rarity. Although most sightings have been of lone or paired whales, schools of up to eight have also been recorded.

Nothing is known of gestation period, length at birth or weaning, nor of peak mating or calving times. However, the species has been recorded in southern African waters only in summer, suggesting that some animals may well so migrate.

Pygmy right whales, unlike right whales, are difficult to spot: even their dorsal fins seldom appear above the surface.

Minke Whale

Balaenoptera acutorostrata

TYPE: Baleen whale – rorqual
(Family Balaenopteridae)
MAXIMUM LENGTH: 10 m
MAXIMUM WEIGHT: 3 t
CONSERVATION STATUS: Not enough is
known; the world population probably runs to
several hundred thousand.

Description

Minke whales are the smallest of the rorquals (the collective name for members of this family), reaching a maximum length of some 10 m in mature females and 9 m in males. The head is sharply pointed, with a distinctive triangular V shape when viewed from above and one very prominent ridge running down its centre. The dorsal fin is prominent and erect. The baleen is mostly a yellowish white, with thin black stripes in certain areas.

The entire upper surface of the body and head is dark grey, becoming paler as the sides merge with the pure white throat, belly and underside of the flukes. Generally, the 'face' of the minke whale is much darker than that of the Bryde's whale. There may be a light grey band across the flipper, and some animals display a whitish 'chevron' on the back, just behind the head and in front of the dorsal fin. The species can be fairly easily distinguished from the Bryde's whale by its coloration in combination with its small size and distinctly triangular head.

Minke whales are inquisitive, often approaching ships and boats closely, turning on their sides as they swim past. The first sign of its presence is a spectacular breach, clear of the water.

Where and when to view

Minke whales occur in all latitudes of the Indian Ocean, from the Antarctic to the tropics, and can be seen anywhere along the southern African coast. The best localities are the same as those for Bryde's whales.

Biology

Little is known of the migratory habits of minke whales, though most adults appear to migrate to the Antarctic during summer. Some, however, especially females and their calves, seem to stay in the warmer waters of our region. In the Antarctic, they feed on krill and copepod crustaceans, in warmer waters (apparently) on fish and crustaceans; Killer whales are known to hunt them; indeed, they seem to form a significant part of the killer whale's diet in the Antarctic.

The average age at sexual maturity, of both female and male, is about eight years. In the warmer waters north of the Antarctic, mating and birthing peak in mid-winter. A single, 2.7-m calf (though twins and triplets have been recorded) is born after a gestation period of about 11 months.

North of the Antarctic, minke whales are commonly encountered singly, in pairs, or in small groups of two or three whales. In the Antarctic feeding grounds, however, they gather into groups, often of more than 100 individuals. The groups are frequently segregated into male and female sub-groups.

As with all marine mammals, dive duration varies with activity, but minke whales often remain underwater for up to five minutes. They generally swim slowly, but are capable of speeds of around 30 km/hour when chased. Their numbers in the Antarctic have expanded dramatically, possibly because the larger whale species have declined. Consequently, whalers have targeted the species in recent years, and there is continuing pressure from whaling countries to allow exploitation of minke whales in the Antarctic.

Minke whales are usually seen in small groups.

Blue Whale

Balaenoptera musculus

TYPE: Baleen whale – rorqual (Family Balaenopteridae)
MAXIMUM LENGTH: 33 m
MAXIMUM WEIGHT: 100 t
CONSERVATION STATUS: Endangered. The total world population is probably less than 10 000, down from somewhere around 400 000 before whaling for the species began.

Description

The blue whale can reach 33 m (pygmy blues: 21 m), though generally grows to only 26 m. Females are larger than males. The head is broad, the snout rounded, the body dark bluish-grey mottled with light grey blotches. The head and lower jaws are uniformly dark, the belly and sides paler than the back. The underside of the flipper is characteristically white.

Where and when to view

This species generally occurs in deep waters and is seldom seen anywhere close to shore.

Biology

Blue whales, like many cetaceans, occur in two forms – the normal and the pygmy – and the information provided here is relevant to both. The species is found in all the oceans but seldom in the tropics. In the waters of the southern hemisphere, it summers in the Antarctic and winters at latitudes above 20 °S. It feeds only in summer, exclusively on krill, filtering more than a ton of this crustacean each day. It occurs singly or in groups of two to three (but occasionally up to 12). It is not a deep diver, usually diving for less than 10 minutes. Swimming speed is generally less than 18 km/h, with short bursts of up to 35 km/h. Blue whales make both high-frequency and very loud, low-frequency moaning sounds.

Mating and calving occur between May and July. A single calf, 7-8 m long, is born after a gestation period of 11 months and is suckled for some seven months, gaining about 100 kg per day. It is 16 m long when it is weaned.

Fin Whale

Balaenoptera physalus

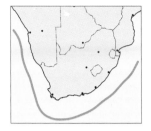

TYPE: Baleen whale – rorqual (Family Balaenopteridae)
MAXIMUM LENGTH: 27 m
MAXIMUM WEIGHT: 70 t
CONSERVATION STATUS: Vulnerable.

Description

Fin whales are slender, elongated, with a streamlined, pointed head and a relatively large dorsal fin three-quarters the way down the body. The back and top of the head are dark grey, the sides lighter and the belly and fluke undersides white. The right side of the head is lighter than the left, and the sides of the lower jaws are also differently coloured, the left dark grey, the right whitish grey.

Where and when to view

The species generally occurs in deep waters and is seldom seen anywhere close to shore.

Biology

Fin whales occur in all the oceans, but are rare in tropical waters. They summer in the polar regions, migrating to the temperate ones in winter to mate and calve. They do not seem to feed in winter and are thin on returning to the Antarctic, but rapidly gain weight from their krill intake in summer. In winter they occur singly or in groups of two or three; in summer they may gather in large numbers to feed. When feeding, they often swim left side upmost, facing the krill swarms with their paler right side – which possibly provides camouflage. They dive relatively deeply (to 200 m or more), spending four to 15 minutes, occasionally 30 minutes, underwater. They utter loud moaning sounds underwater and sometimes also when they surface.

The gestation period is 11 months; the newborn are 6.5 m long, 1.9 t in weight, and are suckled for about seven months, at which time they have reached a length of some 12 m. The calving interval is two years; longevity 30 to 40 years. Like most baleen whales, adult females are bigger than adult males.

Sei Whale

Balaenoptera borealis

TYPE: Baleen whale – rorqual
(Family Balaenopteridae)
MAXIMUM LENGTH: 21 m
MAXIMUM WEIGHT: 55 t
CONSERVATION STATUS: Vulnerable.
There are few reliable size estimates of sei whale populations. However, it is known that their numbers were greatly reduced by commercial exploitation, though they were not important to whalers until the 1960s (mainly because they were smaller and yielded less oil than blue or fin whales). Nevertheless, at least 100 000 were taken between 1961 and 1979.

Description
The form and colour of the species are similar to those of the blue and fin whales. The body is slender and streamlined – but more robust than that of the fin whale, the flippers small and pointed (smaller than a fin whale's), the dorsal fin erect and set two-thirds the way down the body, farther forward and relatively larger than that of either the fin or blue whale. The entire head and back is dark grey to black to bluish and may appear mottled. The flanks are slightly lighter and the belly pale grey to white.

Where and when to view
This species generally occurs in deep waters and is seldom seen anywhere close to shore.

Biology
Sei whales occur in the warm and temperate waters of all the oceans. In the southern hemisphere, they summer in the Antarctic, moving northwards, in autumn, to waters off both the east and west coasts of southern Africa, remaining there from April to October. They generally occur singly or in pairs; larger numbers sometimes aggregate in the feeding grounds. Sei whales capture their prey (krill) by skimming close to the sea surface. They are shallow divers, rarely staying submerged for more than four minutes. Swimming speed is usually around 10 km/h, though when disturbed they can attain 30 km/h.

The species seems to breed year-round, but June is the peak period. After an 11- to 12-month gestation period, a single, 4.6-m calf is born; is suckled for five to nine months and weaned when about 8.5 m long. Females are larger than males; longevity is about 60 years. Indeed the Sei whale is among the fastest swimmers of all cetaceans.

The sei whale, a deep-water and seldom seen species, has a streamlined though fairly robust body.

Bryde's Whale

Balaenoptera edeni

TYPE: Baleen whale – rorqual
(Family Balaenopteridae)
MAXIMUM LENGTH: 15 m
MAXIMUM WEIGHT: 14 t
CONSERVATION STATUS: Not enough is known
about the species to determine its status, though
it is suspected that it may be Endangered,
Vulnerable or Rare. World population numbers
are also unknown.

Where and when to view

Bryde's whales can be seen anywhere along the
length of the southern African coast. The best
viewing sites are capes and promontories. This is
especially so on the east coast during autumn
and early winter, when shoals of small fish are
plentiful inshore and easily spotted by the diving
gannets associated with them.

Description

When observed at sea, Bryde's whales look similar to and are
very difficult to tell from such other rorquals as minke and sei
whales. They are most likely to be confused with the minkes
because both have prominent dorsal fins. If one gets a closer
look at a beached Bryde's specimen, though, there are several
identifying features, the most diagnostic the three ridges
running along the top jaw. Both Bryde's and minke whales can
be seen feeding on large shoals of fish in company with diving
gannets, penguins and frenzied dolphins. Both species are also
distinguished by their feeding patterns. Minke whales swim
rapidly at the surface, on the perimeter of the shoals, taking the
fish on the outside; Bryde's whales on the other hand lunge up
through the shoals, sometimes exposing the whole head, with
the mouth massively distended, and scattering any penguins and
gannets in the way.

The upper body of the Bryde's whale is dark grey and often
has a 'blotched' appearance. Towards the belly the colour
lightens, becoming white in the middle. The head also has a
dark grey upper surface, becoming paler ventrally, though there
is a slate-grey band across the underside of the body at the end
of the throat grooves. The baleen is dark at the corners of the
mouth, white towards the jaw tips. The dorsal fin is large and
upright in relation to the body, making the animal more
reminiscent of a huge dolphin than a whale. Like all baleen
whales, mature females are bigger on average than mature males
(14 m and 13.5 m respectively).

Bryde's whales occur off both the east and west coasts.

Biology

Little is known. Off the southern African coast there appear to be two populations, or stocks. One is apparently 'resident' (non-migratory) in inshore, shallow waters, where shoals of small fish are likely to be abundant. The second appears to be an offshore stock, possibly undertaking seasonal migrations and occurring here only in spring and summer. Although Bryde's whales from elsewhere are known to feed on small crustaceans (euphausiids) and small shoaling fish, the inshore 'residents' seem to feed exclusively on such small shoaling fish as pilchards and anchovies.

Bryde's whales are usually seen singly, although small groups may form during feeding. They are not particularly fast swimmers, attaining speeds similar to those of humpback and minke whales, but they can move quickly when disturbed. Equally, they are not deep divers, usually spending no more than about two minutes underwater, although dives as long as four minutes have been recorded.

In the North Pacific, Bryde's whales have a definite breeding season and, though very little is known of their reproductive cycle in this area, the 'resident' stock presumably mates and gives birth here. After a gestation period of about a year, the female gives birth to a single, 4-m calf, which she suckles during the following year. She then mates again.

This species has been exploited only to a limited extent, and as far as is known none of the Bryde's whale populations have suffered serious depletion.

Humpback Whale

Megaptera novaeangliae

TYPE: Rorqual (baleen whale)
MAXIMUM LENGTH: 12 to 14 m
MAXIMUM WEIGHT: 40 t
CONSERVATION STATUS:
Vulnerable; the population is recovering, but it is
not yet certain that the species is out of danger.

Description

The most striking feature of the humpback
whale, both in and out of the water, is its extremely long
flippers – they are almost one third of the body length and
normally, in contrast to the black upper body surface, white in
colour. The under surface is also black, but may have white
patches. The body is quite short and relatively rotund, the head
large and surmounted by three irregular rows of pronounced
knobs. There are similar projections on the side of each lower
jaw, and at the tip of the lower jaw there is a large rough wart-
like area. The dorsal fin is usually short, thick, low and set upon
a long, gradually sloping hump (hence the common name).
Humpback whales are known to reach 18 m in length,
although the southern hemisphere animals are generally
smaller, the females reaching 13.7 m, the males 13.1 m.

Humpback whales often display a characteristic diving
pattern in which the tail flukes are held vertical and clear of the
water. In most animals the underside of the flukes has a distinctive white and black pattern, which can identify individuals.

Where and when to view

In summer the species feeds in Antarctic waters, some
migrating, in autumn, up the east coast of Africa to 'winter' –
mate and give birth – in the tropical waters off Mozambique
and southern Madagascar.

Unless one is fortunate enough to see them at sea, they are
(usually) only observable from coastal headlands (Robberg
peninsula, Plettenberg Bay) or capes (Knysna Heads) during
these migrations. The northward movement begins in April or
May, their numbers peaking during June and July – which are
the best viewing months. They begin their return journey in
spring (late August, peaking in September); most are back in
the Antarctic by December.

Biology

Humpback whales apparently do not feed
while in tropical waters. In the Antarctic they
live almost exclusively on krill, a small crustacean. By contrast, the diet of the northern
hemisphere animals includes fish, crustaceans
and squid. When feeding, they swim on their
sides, with the mouth open, straining the water
through the baleen. Another typical pattern,
evident in the northern hemisphere, is the 'bubble net', in
which one or more whales will swim around a shoal of fish,
emitting a stream of bubbles from their blowholes. The bubbles act as a kind of 'corral', concentrating or 'herding' the fish
into a tight ball into which the whales lunge.

After a gestation period of between 11 and 12 months, the
female gives birth to a single calf (although twins are not
unknown), which is around 4.2 m in length and is suckled for
10 to 11 months before it is weaned. The female then falls
pregnant again. Females reach sexual maturity when they are
about 12 m long, and are larger than mature males. Much of
the spectacular behaviour associated with humpback whales –

*Humpback whales are renowned for their dramatic breaching
behaviour, lifting their bodies well above the water.*

The characteristic diving pattern of the humpback whale. The flukes are distinctively patterned.

the huge jumps, often clear of the water (breaching), re-entry splashes, smacking the surface with their tails (lobtailing) – are thought to be associated, though not exclusively, with mating.

The humpback whale is also well known for the underwater sounds it produces, an assortment of moans and screams of varied pitch and lasting up to 30 minutes. These 'songs', which differ according to locality, are distinctive and appear to 'evolve' (the patterns gradually change) from year to year. Scientists have therefore speculated that the sounds are a form of communication between whales of the same stock.

Humpbacks occur singly or in small groups, though they may form larger ones where food is concentrated. Diving whales can remain submerged for up to 15 minutes; the average is six or seven minutes. Swimming speed is generally less than 12 km/h, although, when chased by whalers, speeds of up to 25 km/h have been recorded.

Because it occurs close to the coast and swims slowly, the species has been locally hunted for centuries, but the depredation remained relatively modest until the advent of modern whaling methods a few decades ago – explosive harpoons and fast catcher boats. The animals were particularly vulnerable during their migration, and on the breeding grounds. Whaling was especially intensive off Africa's coasts until about 1940, when the second world war intervened. The beleaguered stock received full protection only in 1963, by which time the numbers had been reduced dramatically. Fortunately, recent research by Peter Best (of the Whale Research Unit) suggests that the numbers are increasing.

Sperm Whale

Physeter macrocephalus

TYPE: Toothed whale
(Suborder Odontoceti, Family Physeteridae)
MAXIMUM LENGTH:
12 m (females) to 18 m (males)
MAXIMUM WEIGHT: 57 t
CONSERVATION STATUS: There is insufficient
information, though it is suspected that this
species may be Endangered, Vulnerable or Rare.

Description

The body is relatively short and robust, with a
massive, deep, blunt head that accounts for up to
one-third the total length. The blowhole is on
the left side, at the tip of the snout so that whale
produces a characteristic 'forward' and angled
blow. The lower jaws are narrow and inconspicuous beneath the head. The dorsal fin is a low
hump of variable size and set about two-thirds
down the body from the front of the head, generally with several
smaller humps behind the fin. Flippers are wide and short, with
broadly rounded tips. The flukes are broad, with a deep central
notch. The upper part of the flanks are often markedly wrinkled,
particularly in the middle portion of the body.

Colour is generally a uniform dark grey-blue, becoming
slightly paler towards the lower surface, with lighter, often white
lips. In both sexes each lower jaw carries 18 to 30 large conical
teeth, though some may not have erupted. The upper jaws may
contain up to 18 small, rudimentary teeth although, again, they
are not always erupted.

Where and when to view

Very seldom observed from shore, but can sometimes be seen
from the 'Gates' at Port St Johns.

Biology

In the late 18th and much of the 19th centuries several hundred
whaling ships, many of them American, voyaged the world's
oceans in search of sperm whales. Many adventure novels have
been written about the subject, the best known probably
Herman Melville's *Moby Dick*, a book based on the author's
experience of the protracted hunt for a legendary giant white
sperm whale. Until the mid-1970s many thousands of sperm
whales were killed in South African waters and this afforded
opportunities for research, so rather more is known about this
species than about most other cetaceans.

Sperm whales inhabit all the oceans, occurring from the
equator to the edge of the polar pack ice. However, they show
a preference for deep water and rarely venture over the continental shelf. In the Indian Ocean, they are found as far north as

*Sperm whales occur everywhere from the polar regions to the
tropics, but are rarely seen from shore.*

Adult males are often solitary creatures; the females and younger individuals form large groups.

the Arabian Gulf. There are no estimates of the numbers off southern Africa, but it is reckoned that about 32 000 occur within the Southern Ocean Sanctuary.

Other than large males, which are mostly solitary, sperm whales are social, associating in either breeding or bachelor groups. The former, which may be 200-strong, contain females of all ages together with immature and younger (pubertal) males. Sexually mature males join these groups only during the winter breeding season. Bachelor groups, containing 20 or so whales, consist entirely of older, sexually mature males of similar age and size. Males will mix with females, but only for short periods as they 'search' for mates.

Generally speaking, sperm whales migrate northwards into the South Atlantic and Indian oceans in autumn, returning south in spring. Females and small males appear off the Cape West and KwaZulu-Natal coasts in February and are at their most numerous in April. Medium-sized and large males reach peak numbers a month or two later. Nevertheless, some sperm whales can be found in tropical waters throughout the year.

Though sperm whales often remain motionless at the surface, they are excellent divers. Young whales dive for only short periods (about 20 minutes), but an adult male can submerge for nearly two hours to depths of more than 2 000 m. The species feeds almost entirely on deep-sea squids (sometimes 2 to 3 m long), but also takes fish, skates and sharks. It appears these whales consume 3 to 4 per cent of their body weight each day.

The species' lifespan is 60 to 70 years; females reach sexual maturity at 10 years; 4-m long calves are born around March after a gestation period of almost 15 months and are suckled for several years, the female calving every three to six years.

Pygmy Sperm Whale

Kogia breviceps

TYPE: Toothed whale
(Suborder Odontoceti, Family Kogiidae)
MAXIMUM LENGTH: 3.4 m
MAXIMUM WEIGHT: 400 kg
CONSERVATION STATUS:
Insufficient information.

Description

Both the pygmy and dwarf sperm whales are small, similar in form and colour, robust, with a short, rounded head which is about one-sixth of the total length. The head projects beyond the lower jaws and the blowhole is slightly to the left of the midline. The mouth is small, the lower jaws set with long, curved and very sharp teeth. The dorsal fin is small and set slightly more than halfway down the body from the snout. Both these sperm whale species are dark bluish to grey over the back, top of the head and flukes and the outer surface of the flipper. The coloration changes to a paler blue-grey on the sides, shading into a white or pale grey on the under surface, flippers and flukes. The sides of the snout, from the tip to behind the eye, are light grey with, sometimes, a blackish patch around the eye. The under surface extends up in front of the flipper in a narrow band behind.

Maximum size and body profile are the features that most easily distinguish the two species. The head of the pygmy sperm whale, like that of the sperm whale, is square rather than round, the dorsal fin smaller and more hooked.

Where and when to view

Unless stranded, the pygmy sperm whale is unlikely to be seen. It is oceanic and generally sighted to the seaward side of the continental shelf.

Biology

There is no information on the abundance of this species. However, like the dwarf sperm whale, the high frequency of strandings indicates that it may be relatively common along both the east and west coasts of the southern African region. Swimming speed is generally less than 18 km/h, with short bursts of up to 35 km/h. Females are sexually mature when they attain a length of 2.6 m. The gestation period is not known. Calves are about 1.2 m long when they are born.

The species is distinguished by its squarish head.

Dwarf sperm whale

Kogia simus

TYPE: Toothed whale
(Suborder Odontoceti, Family Kogiidae)
MAXIMUM LENGTH: 2.7 m
MAXIMUM WEIGHT: 210 kg
CONSERVATION STATUS: Insufficiently known.

Description
See pygmy sperm whale. Smaller than the pygmy sperm whale (see maximum lengths) and has fewer teeth: only 8 to 11 small, but robust, sharp teeth in each lower jaw, as opposed to 12 to 16 less robust teeth.

Where and when to view
Unless stranded, the dwarf sperm whale is unlikely to be seen. It is oceanic and generally sighted at the edge of the continental shelf on both east and southwest coasts.

Biology
Nothing is known of the abundance of these whales, though the high frequency of strandings suggests they are fairly common. Nevertheless, they are seldom seen at sea and, when they are, usually in small groups of four or five animals, though groups of 10 have been recorded.

Dwarf sperm whales feed preferentially on squid and sometimes fish and crustaceans inhabiting the slope or edge of the continental shelf. In this respect, they are more coastal than pygmy sperm whales, but probably still dive to depths in excess of 300 m. The majority of squid taken are light emitting, probably indicating that dwarf sperm whales rely, to some extent, on eyesight to find their prey at depths where light does not penetrate.

Most strandings in our region occur in summer, implying that dwarf sperm whales move inshore during that period. Many of the females stranded in summer have young, suggesting that these whales calve, and probably mate, predominantly in late spring and summer.

Unlike most cetaceans, dwarf and pygmy sperm whales have relatively flaccid flukes (tails), implying that they are slow moving. Another characteristic feature of both species is the small mouth (that is, small by large mammal standards). These facts raise the intriguing question of how dwarf, and pygmy, sperm whales catch their food, most of which appear to be rapid swimmers. Like sperm whales, there is speculation that both dwarf and pygmy sperm whales use loud, high-frequency pulsed sounds to 'stun' the prey they are pursuing. The prey species lies lifeless in the water, allowing the whale to swim up to and consume it.

Males and females attain sexual maturity when they reach about 2.1 m in length; mothers give birth after a gestation period of (it is thought) about one year. Calving appears to occur in spring and summer; the newborn calf is about 1 m long.

Dwarf sperm whales appear to stun their prey with sound.

Arnoux's Beaked Whale

Berardius arnuxii

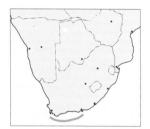

TYPE: Beaked whale
(Suborder Odontoceti, Family Ziphiidae)
MAXIMUM LENGTH: 9.75 m
MAXIMUM WEIGHT: 10 t
CONSERVATION STATUS:
Insufficient information.

Description

This is the largest of the southern hemisphere's beaked whales, attaining a maximum length of almost 10 m. Females are probably larger than males. The body is robust, but the bulbous head appears small, with a prominent beak, the lower jaw protruding well beyond the upper. In both males and females, two teeth project from the tip of each lower jaw; the front pair are larger (up to 7 cm high). The flippers are small; the small dorsal fin is set two-thirds of the body length from the snout. The flukes are broad and do not have a central notch. The coloration of the upper surfaces is dark grey to black, becoming paler underneath.

Where and when to view

Unless stranded, Arnoux's beaked whale is unlikely to be seen.

Biology

This beaked whale is found only in the southern hemisphere, where its distribution is circumpolar; it occurs from cool temperate waters to the Antarctic. All sightings have been in deep oceanic waters, though these whales are sometimes seen in the vicinity of seamounts (underwater mountains). They are shy animals, difficult to observe and identify at sea, and little is known of their biology and behaviour. They are capable of long dives, which often last an hour or more, though most dives last less than 15 minutes. They seem to feed predominantly on squid, but may also take fish. They appear to form small, usually less than ten-strong, schools. However, one group of 80 whales has been recorded. The whale has not suffered extensively from commercial exploitation and, as a result, very little is known of the species' reproductive cycle.

These whales, which inhabit the deeper oceanic waters, are shy and seldom observed. Females are larger than males.

Blainville's Beaked Whale

Mesoplodon densirostris

TYPE: Beaked whale
(Suborder Odontoceti, Family Ziphiidae)
MAXIMUM LENGTH: 4.7 m
MAXIMUM WEIGHT: 1 t
CONSERVATION STATUS:
Insufficient information.

Strandings on South Africa's beaches occur mainly in late summer and winter, though their occurrence elsewhere does not suggest any migratory pattern.

This beaked whale is notable for the pronounced curve of its mouth.

Description

This species is similar in shape to Layard's beaked whale, both sexes reaching a maximum length of about 4.7 m. Unlike the Layard's, however, the head slopes fairly gently and the mouth curves up strongly at its midlength. This upward curve marks the position of a pair of teeth in the lower jaws. In adult males, each fist-sized tooth protrudes at the curve and, in large males, is a striking feature. The dorsal fin is set nearly two-thirds of the body length from the snout. The entire upper surface of the back, head, upper jaw, eye area and the flipper are dark grey, shading to a pale blue-grey on the under surface of the head and chest, but becoming whiter underneath as far as the anus.

Where and when to view

Unless stranded, Blainville's beaked whale is unlikely to be seen.

Biology

Almost nothing is known. Most of the information we have has been gleaned from stranded animals and the very infrequent sightings at sea. Generally, the species is widely distributed in tropical and subtropical waters in both the northern and southern hemispheres. All those observed at sea have been in deeper, offshore waters and most are seen singly or in pairs, though groups of up to seven have been recorded. The animal is known to dive for over 45 minutes, and to feed primarily on squid and some fish.

Layard's Beaked Whale

Mesoplodon layardii

TYPE: Beaked whale
(Suborder Odontoceti, Family Ziphiidae)
MAXIMUM LENGTH: 6.2 m
MAXIMUM WEIGHT: 2 t
CONSERVATION STATUS:
Insufficient information.

Description

Like most beaked whales this, the largest member of the genus Mesoplodon, is a relatively slender animal with a distinct forehead and a long, slender beak. The line of the mouth is fairly straight, interrupted only in adult males, where a pair of 'strap-like' teeth protrude and curve over the upper jaw to meet slightly in front of the forehead – hence the alternative common name 'strap-toothed' whale. A small dorsal fin is set about two-thirds the way down the body. The colour pattern, better known than that of most members of the genus, is complex, the body predominantly dark brownish-grey to black. Much of the underside is a contrasting white, as is the beak and throat. There is also a whitish band around the head, and the back and sides may be spotted with white to light-grey patches.

Where and when to view

Unless stranded, Layard's beaked whale is unlikely to be seen.

Biology

Little is known of the species' biology and behaviour. Although these animals are difficult to approach and observe – they seem deliberately to avoid vessels – sightings at sea suggest that they occur in small schools of up to three individuals. Stomach contents of stranded animals indicate a diet mainly of squid. In southern African waters, specimens strand in summer, suggesting a seasonal occurrence in this area. Calving appears to occur at this time.

The purpose of the male's 'strapped teeth' has puzzled zoologists for years. There must have been some evolutionary trigger, but they seem to be of little use as weapons and, because they severely restrict the mouth's ability to open, may be more of a hindrance than an asset.

Layard's beaked whale is distinguished by a curious pair of strap-like teeth that protrude and curve around the upper jaw.

Hector's Beaked Whale

Mesoplodon hectori

TYPE: Beaked whale
(Suborder Odontoceti, Family Ziphiidae)
MAXIMUM LENGTH: 4.5 m
MAXIMUM WEIGHT: 1 000 kg
CONSERVATION STATUS: Insufficient information.

Description

What information we have on this animal has been gleaned only from strandings (less than 35 specimens worldwide), and it has only been seen alive at sea on a few occasions. Its body colour appears to be a dark grey-brown on the upper surface, with a paler grey on the under surface. Scratches and scars cover the body, and males seem to have white on the underside of the flukes. A single pair of small, flattened, triangular teeth is located near the tip of the lower jaw, erupting in males.

The species is distinguished from other beaked whales only by the skull features. It resembles True's beaked whale in the position of its single pair of teeth, which protrude at an angle from the tip of the upper jaw.

Where and when to view

Unless it becomes stranded, Hector's beaked whale is unlikely to be seen in the region.

Biology

Hector's beaked whale is primarily a southern hemisphere animal which has been reported from South America, South Africa, Australia and New Zealand. Nevertheless it remains almost completely unknown. The paucity of strandings and sea sightings indicate that the species is rare.

Squid remains were found in the stomach of one stranded specimen. Most of the sightings at sea have been of pairs of animals. Male Hector's beaked whales appear to grow to a maximum length of about 4.5 m, slightly longer than females. As far as is known, this species occurs in cool, temperate waters to either side of Latitude 34 °S.

Gray's Beaked Whale

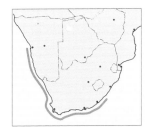

Mesoplodon grayi

TYPE: Beaked whale (Suborder Odontoceti, Family Ziphiidae)
MAXIMUM LENGTH: up to 5.6 m
MAXIMUM WEIGHT: 1.1 t
CONSERVATION STATUS: Insufficient information.

Description

Although it can grow to a length of about 5.6 m, Gray's beaked whale is the most slender member of the genus *Mesoplodon*, and it has the longest and most slender beak of any of family's species. There is one triangular tooth in each lower jaw, about one-third of the mouth's length from the tip of the beak. The teeth are large and only apparent in adult males, although there is a row of up to twenty minute, rudimentary teeth in the upper jaw of both sexes. The dorsal fin is set about two-thirds of the body length from the snout.

The upper surface of the head, back and flukes is dark slate-grey with a hint of brown. The colouring becomes paler on the sides, turning to a light grey on the under surface of the animal's head and body – except for a darker streak down the middle of the belly and a dark outer surface on the flippers. The upper jaw and lips are almost pure white, forming a V as the white slopes down to the eyes.

Where and when to view

Unless stranded, this species is unlikely to be seen.

Biology

Habits and behaviour are not known. Sightings at sea indicate these whales form small groups of four to six individuals. A mass stranding of 28 of these whales has been recorded. They surface in a characteristic fashion: the long, slender jaw is lifted slowly out of the water at a 45° angle, exposing the entire head. Distribution appears to be circumpolar in the southern hemisphere, in waters deeper than 1 800 m. There is no information on numbers, but incidental captures in deep-sea gill nets have been recorded, suggesting that they could be quite common.

True's Beaked Whale

Mesoplodon mirus

TYPE: Beaked whale
(Suborder Odontoceti, Family Ziphiidae)
MAXIMUM LENGTH: 5.3 m
MAXIMUM WEIGHT: 1.4 t
CONSERVATION STATUS: Insufficiently known.

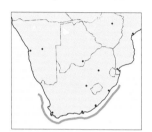

Description

The bodies of True's and Layard's beaked whales have similar proportions, though their heads differ considerably in shape. In True's, the fatty forehead (melon) extends almost to the tip of the beak, making the latter look relatively short, and the line of the mouth curves gently upwards at its midpoint. There is a single pair of teeth at the extreme tip of the lower jaw in both sexes.

In adult males the teeth are large and protrude at an angle in front of the tip of the upper jaw; those of adult females bare-ly erupt. A small, slightly hooked dorsal fin is visible about two-thirds of the way down the body.

Colour patterns have not been conclusively established and there seem to be some differences between northern and southern hemisphere whales. Specimens stranded on South African beaches are generally a dark blue or slate-grey dorsally; the fin and upper surface of the flukes are a smoky grey. This coloration contrasts with the white and light grey of the snout's tip, the throat and the under surface of the body.

Where and when to view

Unless stranded, this species is unlikely to be seen. Even at sea, their behaviour is cryptic: they appear shy of boats and there have been few observations.

Biology

Like most of the region's deep-water whales, little is known of the biology or habits of True's beaked whale. Both squid and fish remains have been found in the stomachs of stranded specimens. Young, still suckling calves are found stranded throughout the year, suggesting that the calving season is extended over several months.

True's beaked whales are known only from the temperate northern Atlantic, western Australia and southeastern southern Africa.

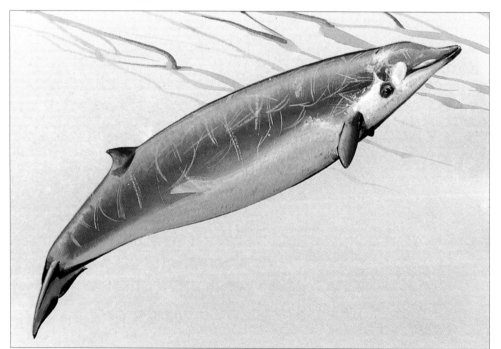

The whale's forehead (or melon) is extended; the beak appears short.

Cuvier's Beaked Whale

Ziphius cavirostris

TYPE: Beaked whale (Suborder Odontoceti, Family Ziphiidae)
MAXIMUM LENGTH: 7.5 m
MAXIMUM WEIGHT: 3 t
CONSERVATION STATUS: Insufficient information.

Description

The body is fairly robust, the head proportionately large, with a distinctive forehead sloping almost to the jaw tip. In mature males, a single tooth erupts at the tip of each bottom jaw. Adult coloration is generally dark on the sides and belly. The lower jaws, throat, forehead and back to about mid-body length, are dark cream. Oval white scars are found on males, possibly from wounds inflicted during fights.

Where and when to view

Unless stranded, this species is unlikely to be seen.

Biology

As with almost all the beaked whales, and most cetaceans for that matter, almost nothing is known of the biology or habits of Cuvier's beaked whale. What is known about the species has been obtained from only several tens of strandings worldwide, a small-scale commercial fishery off Japan, and very infrequent sightings at sea.

Cuvier's beaked whale occurs in all except polar waters. They are most often seen alone, though groups of up to seven have been recorded. Generally, they are cryptic and unobtrusive at sea and there is some evidence that they dive to avoid vessels. The stomachs of stranded animals indicate that they feed on deep-sea fish and squid and are, therefore, probably capable of deep and long dives (some exceeding 40 minutes have been recorded).

The calving season appears to last several months – from summer to autumn. Calves, which at birth are about 2.5 m in length, are born after an unknown gestation period. Sexual maturity is reached when the animals reach 5.5 m in length; males are slightly larger than females.

Southern Bottlenosed Whale

Hyperoodon planifrons

TYPE: Beaked whale (Suborder Odontoceti, Family Ziphiidae)
MAXIMUM LENGTH: 7.8 m
MAXIMUM WEIGHT: 3.5 t
CONSERVATION STATUS: Insufficient information.

Description

This species can be distinguished from other beaked whales by its size and prominent, bulbous forehead. In older animals the latter tends to overhang the short beak. There is a pair of conical teeth at the tip of the lower jaw, which, even in adult males, hardly project above the gum. The flippers are small; the flukes broad and lacking a central notch. A large dorsal fin is set well back on the body and, although it is almost triangular, the tip projects backwards. The animal is variously reported to be cloud-grey, bluish-black or brown, the colour becoming lighter with age. Five whales sighted about 800 km south of Cape Town were a dark fawn with a hint of grey.

Where and when to view

Unless stranded, this species is unlikely to be seen.

Biology

Few specimens have been examined, and these whales are generally shy and unapproachable, making sea observations difficult. As a result, little is known of their biology or behaviour. Sightings show they occur mostly in small schools of less than 10 individuals, though groups of up to 25 have been seen.

This is a cold-water whale, occurring throughout the southern oceans south of about 30 °S. It appears to feed predominantly on squid and, perhaps, krill, and it is a deep diver, able to stay submerged for over an hour. One of the few whales examined had more than 50 growth-layers in its teeth, suggesting the species may have a lifespan of more than 50 years.

There is some evidence of another, similar looking species of bottlenosed whale, but neither specimens nor photographs have yet been produced.

Killer Whale

Orcinus orca

TYPE: Toothed whale – dolphin
MAXIMUM LENGTH: 10 m
MAXIMUM WEIGHT: 10 t
CONSERVATION STATUS: Insufficiently known; although it is suspected that this species may be Endangered, Vulnerable or Rare, there is not enough information available to place it in any of these categories.

Description

The killer whale, or orca, is a robust dolphin with a short, rounded head ending in a very short beak that contains 10 to 13 large, conical teeth in each jaw. The flippers are broad and well rounded at the tips. Mature killer whales are easily distinguished by their large dorsal fins which grow in height as the animal gets older. In mature females the fin may be up to l m in height, in old males almost 2 m. These large dolphins have broad flukes (tails), which are proportionately bigger in males than in females. The dark, black to brownish colour of the upperparts and sides of the body contrast quite strongly with the white of the lower jaw and belly. Behind the eye there is an oval white patch, with another patch, sometimes more grey than white, behind the dorsal fin. In some animals, the patches behind the dorsal fin appear joined to form a saddle.

Adult male killer whales reach a maximum length of 10 m and adult females a length of 7.5 m.

The killer whale, like the dolphins, uses echolocation to find its prey.

Where and when to view

Killer whales can be seen anywhere along the southern African coast. Unfortunately their appearances are unpredictable and, though sightings are often reported (particularly from Plettenberg and Algoa bays), these are irregular.

Biology

Killer whales are distributed worldwide, occurring in the coastal and offshore waters in both tropical and polar seas, though they appear to be more abundant in cooler waters. Little is known of their migratory patterns, but their movements are probably determined by the migrations of their prey.

Killer whales form groups of up to 200 animals though, in the southern African region, groups tend to be much smaller, often no more than three or four whales. They can attain speeds of 30 km/h, and dive for periods of up to six or seven minutes.

Otherwise known as the orca, the killer whale hunts in packs, its prey comprising small whales, dolphins, seals, fish and squid.

Killer whales, like all dolphins, produce both whistling and clicking sounds. The former is probably used for communication with other group members, the latter for echolocating prey, and, perhaps, also for communication. The effect the sounds have on other marine animals can be dramatic, prompting whales and other dolphins to flee the area, and penguins and seals to head as quickly as they can for the safety of land. The sight of them 'popping' from the water, as if the sea were boiling, is a comical one – but, to the penguins and seals, it is a deadly serious exercise in survival.

In tropical waters, killer whales appear to mate and calve throughout the year; in the cooler areas these processes are probably restricted to the warmer months. The gestation period is about 12 months; calves are about 2.3 m long at birth, and are suckled for about a year, though they may continue suckling for social reasons for much longer. Killer whales reach sexual maturity, and a length of some 5 m, at about 12 years of age.

The diet of this species is varied, embracing fish, squid, sea birds and other marine mammals such as seals, dolphins and small whales. Accounts record that killer whale packs disable their mammal prey by biting the flippers or flukes, and then attempt to get to the tongue, which they appear to savour. Seals seem to have an inborn fear of the animal, which has a reputation as a voracious eater. In one instance, the stomach of a killer whale was reliably reported to contain the remains of 14 seals and 13 porpoises! Notwithstanding this, recent investigations have shown that some forms do not prey on marine mammals. In northern Canada, two 'races', or types, of killer whale live side by side, one migratory, the other resident. The former regularly eats other marine mammals as part of its diet, the latter eats only fish. There is little research on the species in southern Africa, and the 'race' of orca inhabiting our waters is unknown, although it is reported that the animals chase dolphins and seals.

Despite their reputation and apparent ferocity, there are no authenticated accounts of unprovoked, wild killer whale attacks on man. In captivity, however, though they appear docile and seem to respond well to training, there are numerous reports of trainers being killed or injured by these huge animals.

Pygmy Killer Whale

Feresa attenuata

TYPE: Toothed whale – dolphin
(Suborder Odontoceti, Family Delphinidae)
MAXIMUM LENGTH: 2.7 m
MAXIMUM WEIGHT: 225 kg
CONSERVATION STATUS:
Insufficient information.

Description

Pygmy killer whales are similar in appearance to
melon-headed whales. The body is slender, with a rounded head
and no beak. The body tapers noticeably behind the dorsal fin,
which is relatively large. So too are the flippers, which are
rounded at the tips. There is a narrow groove down the midline
of the chest and belly, from the flippers to about two–thirds of
the way down the body. The overall colour is blue-black, with
lighter greyish flanks extending from eye to tail. The chest is
grey and there is a white area on the belly at mid
length. The lips are whitish in colour. Females
are smaller than males, attaining a maximum
length of 2.4 m. There are 8 to 10 teeth in each
upper jaw, and 11 to 13 in each lower jaw.

Where and when to view

This species seldom ventures close to shore,
though it can be seen on the outer, fringing reefs
of some of the oceanic islands in the western Indian Ocean, and
in areas where deep, submarine canyons occur close inshore
(possibly off Port St Johns).

Biology

The species is widely distributed in tropical and subtropical
waters, and is found off both the east and west coasts of southern Africa. Little is known of its
biology or behaviour. It occurs
mostly in small groups (fewer
than 50 individuals) though
larger ones of up to several
hundred have been reported. It
feeds predominantly on fish and
squid and has been reported to
attack and eat other dolphins
(hence the common name).
Compared with the melon-
headed whale, the animal seems
slow and lethargic, though
when herding other dolphins it
apparently swims at some speed.
Whether the species migrates, or
is resident in areas where it is
found, remains unknown.

*These animals feed mainly on
squid and fish, but have been
known to attack other dolphins.*

False Killer Whale

Pseudorca crassidens

TYPE: Toothed whale – dolphin
(Suborder Odontoceti, Family Delphinidae)
MAXIMUM LENGTH: 6 m
MAXIMUM WEIGHT: 2 t
CONSERVATION STATUS:
Insufficient information.

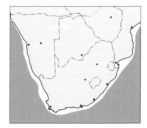

Description

The false killer whale has a bluntly rounded head which, in profile, is less deep than that of the killer whale and similar to that of the pygmy killer whale. The teeth are conical and pointed at their tips; the flippers quite small and pointed, with a 'boomerang'-shaped leading edge. The dorsal fin is relatively small and is set at the body's mid length. The colour is generally black, perhaps with a brownish tinge, and sometimes there is a lighter mid-ventral streak. The female is smaller than the male, attaining a length of 4.5 m. There are between seven and 12 teeth in each jaw.

Where and when to view

The species seldom ventures close to shore, though it can be seen on the outer, fringing reefs of some of the oceanic islands in the western Indian Ocean, and in areas where deep submarine canyons occur close to the coast – for example off Toliara in Madagascar, where they come within 500 m of the shoreline.

Biology

This species is widely distributed in all seas except the polar regions, occurring off both the east and west coasts of southern Africa – apparently in summer in the southern parts, year-round farther north. One of its more interesting features is that it occasionally strands en masse. Three mass strandings (of 100, 300 and 58 whales), have been reported off the Western Cape coast.

These are fast-moving animals, often leaping clear of the water and behaving more like the smaller dolphins. Group sizes range between about 10 and 50, though much larger ones have

been observed. The species feeds predominantly on squid and fish and is known to steal from the long-lines of fishermen. Indications are that it is an oceanic feeder, either diving deep by day or feeding on squid that move towards the surface at night. The false killer whale makes echolocatory clicking sounds, and has been heard to utter a wavering, whistling noise.

False killer whales move quickly through the water in search of the fish and squid that comprise their diet.

Melon-headed Whale

Peponocephala electra

TYPE: Toothed whale – dolphin
(Suborder Odontoceti, Family Delphinidae)
MAXIMUM LENGTH: 2.75 m
MAXIMUM WEIGHT: 275 kg
CONSERVATION STATUS: Insufficiently known.

Description

Even to the trained eye, melon-headed whales are easily confused with pygmy killer whales: they are of similar size and appearance.

However, on close inspection, the two can be distinguished from each other. Melon-headed whales have pointed flippers, a large number of smaller teeth and a black, triangular 'mask' on the face; pygmy killer whales, on the other hand, have rounded flippers, fewer and more robust teeth and a more uniform coloration. Young and female melon-headed whales also have a short, though poorly defined, beak.

Melon-headed whales are generally charcoal grey to black, with white lips and a white patch about three-quarters the way along the belly. A lighter coloured stripe widens as it runs from the blowhole down to the snout tip. There are 20 to 25 small, slender teeth in each jaw.

Where and when to view

The species seldom ventures close to shore, though it can be seen on the outer, fringing reefs of some of the oceanic islands in the western Indian Ocean, and in areas where deep, submarine canyons occur close inshore.

Biology

Melon-headed whales occur in warm, tropical and subtropical waters and there are few records from the southern African region, other than one or two sightings from the Mozambique Channel and a live animal stranded at Hout Bay (probably at the limit of its range). As a result, very little is known of the species' biology or behaviour in this area.

Melon-headed whales are highly social and generally occur in groups of between 100 and 500 (though a group of 2 000 has been observed), and are often seen swimming with other cetaceans. They often move at high speed, 'porpoising' as they do so. They enthusiastically ride the bow-waves of passing vessels and will even displace other dolphin species to secure position. They are known to feed on squid and small fish.

The melon-headed whale, a sociable species, swims quickly, often breaking the surface in a cloud of spray. It occurs in largish groups.

Short-finned Pilot Whale

Globicephala macrorhynchus

TYPE: Toothed whale – dolphin
(Suborder Odontoceti, Family Delphinidae)
MAXIMUM LENGTH: 6 m
MAXIMUM WEIGHT: 3.6 t
CONSERVATION STATUS:
Insufficient information

Description

This species is similar in form and appearance to the long-finned pilot whale. However, the two species can be distinguished by their coloration, by the number of teeth and flipper length. Unlike long-finned pilot whales, the short-finned species may have an almost white 'saddle' behind the dorsal fin; only seven to nine sharply pointed teeth in each jaw, and flippers that are usually less than one-fifth of the body length. Overall colour is brownish-black, with an indistinct dark grey patch on the throat and, in some animals, the whitish 'saddle' described. Adult males are slightly bigger than adult females.

Where and when to view

In the southern African region the species occurs in warmer waters, predominantly off the east coast. Nevertheless it is a deep-water species and unlikely to be seen close inshore. Although frequent sightings of 'pilot whales' are reported from Plettenberg Bay, it is unclear which species these refer to.

Biology

Very little is known about these animals in our region. Although they readily approach vessels at sea, they tend not to remain close for very long and observation is difficult. Short-finned pilot whales are highly social and are almost never seen alone; school sizes range from three to several hundred individuals. Like the long-finned species, schools appear to be bound by strong social bonds, probably functioning as matriarchal groups (relatively small ones, of up to 25 individuals, in southern African waters) led by an older female and consisting of her female relatives (aunts, sisters and daughters) – a structure curiously similar to that of elephant herds.

Although they take fish, short-finned pilot whales are considered to be predominantly squid eaters.

This whale is distinguished from its long-finned cousin by, among other things, the white 'saddle' behind its dorsal fin. It is a highly social animal, living in groups led by a matriarch.

Long-finned Pilot Whale

Globicephala melas

TYPE: Toothed whale – dolphin
(Suborder Odontoceti, Family Delphinidae)
MAXIMUM LENGTH: 6.7 m
MAXIMUM WEIGHT: 2 t
CONSERVATION STATUS:
Insufficient information.

Description

Pilot whales are robust animals with bulbous foreheads that overhang very short, broad beaks. The mouth is inclined upwards and backwards, set with a row of teeth in the front of each jaw. The dorsal fin is elongated and low, the flippers tapered and long (generally more than one-fifth body length). Overall, the animal is a dark brownish-black, with a greyish-white patch on the throat and a white streak down the midline of the belly. In some animals, particularly in the southern hemisphere, there is a whitish streak behind the eye and a whitish saddle behind the dorsal fin. Males are slightly larger than females (6.7 m and 5.7 m respectively) and there are eight to 12 sharp, conical teeth in each jaw.

Where and when to view

Within our region the species occurs only in more temperate, colder waters from Namibia around to the Eastern Cape. Nevertheless, it is a deep-water species and is unlikely to be seen close inshore.

Biology

More is known about the biology and behaviour of this species than about those of many other whales and dolphins. They are highly social, occurring in groups numbering from 20 to 1 000 individuals. The groups are apparently quite stable, possibly comprising extended family groups, though the mating system is probably polygynous. This tight social structure has encouraged several whaling enterprises to establish 'drive' fisheries, where schools of pilot whales are driven onto beaches for slaughter. Like false killer whales, the animals are often involved in mass strandings.

Long-finned pilot whales are deep divers and often forage in a broad phalanx, sometimes with other species of dolphin, to hunt squid (which is their principal prey). Occasionally they have been seen performing aerial acrobatics but more often they are observed rafting (apparently resting) at the surface.

This is a deep-water species, rarely seen close inshore, though there are several records of mass strandings.

76

Rough-toothed Dolphin

Steno bredanensis

TYPE: Toothed whale – dolphin
(Suborder Odontoceti, Family Delphinidae)
MAXIMUM LENGTH: 2.8 m
MAXIMUM WEIGHT: up to 160 kg
CONSERVATION STATUS:
Insufficient information.

Description

This species is fairly robust and, superficially,
looks very similar to the bottlenose dolphin. However, the head
is conical and, unlike all other dolphins, there is no distinct
boundary (apex) between the head and the beak, giving the
animal a slightly reptilian appearance. The flippers are large –
they seem oversized for the body – and set quite far back on the
side. The dorsal fin is almost upright
and not hooked. The upper third of
the body is a dark bluish-grey that dips
down on the sides, below the dorsal
fin. Overall, coloration becomes lighter
on the flanks, the paleness progressing
to the belly, which is white, as are the
lips and much of the lower jaw. White
scars and spots often cover much of
the body. There are 20 to 27 teeth in
each jaw; the jaws have subtle, but
detectable, vertical ridges, giving the
species its common name.

Where and when to view

This is essentially a deep-water, tropical
species and there are few records
from southern Africa. Rough-toothed
dolphins are unlikely to be seen in the
region unless stranded.

*An inhabitant of the world's deeper
and warmer waters, the rough-toothed
dolphin has seldom been seen in the
southern African region.*

Biology

Rough-toothed dolphins are seen mostly in
groups of between 10 and 20, but schools of
over 100 have been reported. They tend to be
lethargic, but will occasionally ride the bow-
waves of ocean-going vessels. When swimming
at high speed, they will often keep the head and
chin at the surface, skimming the water in a
characteristic behaviour described as 'surfing'.
Reports indicate that they sometimes associate with floating
objects and also with other cetaceans.

These dolphins feed mostly on deep-sea squid and fish,
including large game species, though the remains of some coastal
prey were found in one animal stranded in KwaZulu-Natal.

Spotted Dolphin

Stenella attenuata

TYPE: Toothed whale – dolphin
(Suborder Odontoceti, Family Delphinidae)
MAXIMUM LENGTH: 2.3 m
MAXIMUM WEIGHT: 120 kg
CONSERVATION STATUS:
Insufficient information.

Description

This species is similar in form to spinner and euphrosyne dolphins, though it is slightly larger than the former and more slender than the latter. It has a long, narrow beak; the dorsal fin is set at the body's mid length and is relatively small and hooked. The beak, top of the head, back, dorsal fin, flippers and flukes and the forward part of the flanks are a darkish grey.

The posterior of the flanks and the body's underparts are lighter grey to white. Dark stripes run from the flipper base to the hindmost corner of the mouth, and from the eyes and blowhole to the apex of the forehead. White spots, or flecks, are scattered over the whole body (hence the common name), but predominantly on the flanks. Characteristic features are a white tip to the snout and a whitish blaze (flash) running up from the posterior, underside of the body to the upper surface, just in front of the flukes.

Spotted dolphins off central and northern KwaZulu-Natal appear to be larger and less spotted than those in the more tropical waters of the north. There are between 36 and 45 teeth in each upper and lower jaw.

Where and when to view

These are among the most commonly seen dolphins at sea in the Indian Ocean region north of Cape St Lucia. Unfortunately, though, they seldom venture close to land.

Biology

Spotted dolphins are found in the tropical waters of both the Atlantic and Indian oceans. In our region, the Atlantic spotted dolphin *Stenella frontailis*, which probably occurs off Namibia, is not described here.

The migratory movements of the pantropical spotted dolphin are not known, though it has been observed off northern KwaZulu-Natal and Mozambique throughout the year. It

The spotted dolphin's long beak, and the markings on the adult's body, are distinguishing features.

A quintet of spotted dolphins seen from below. These animals often associate with spinner dolphins.

occurs in large schools, often more than 100-strong. Mixed groups of spotted and spinner dolphins, often of several hundred individuals, have regularly been recorded in the Indian Ocean region, and will readily ride the bow-waves. Groups of both dolphins are often seen in bays and just outside fringing coral reefs and around islands – areas that sustain ample fish prey. They may also use these waters as resting grounds, and to avoid sharks during the daylight hours. Spotted dolphins are fast swimmers, and 'porpoise' when the group is moving at high speed. The species feeds predominantly on such surface-living deep-water prey as flying fish and squid. The gestation period is approximately a year; the newborn calves are about a metre long.

In the past, large numbers of spotted dolphins were accidentally killed by the tuna fishermen of the eastern and central Pacific. Thankfully, the mortality there is now much reduced, but gill-netting and other practices are taking a heavy toll around the Indian Ocean. In some areas, whole schools of dolphins have been driven onto sandbanks and slaughtered.

Fraser's Dolphin

Lagenodelphis hosei

TYPE: Toothed whale – dolphin
(Suborder Odontoceti, Family Delphinidae)
MAXIMUM LENGTH: 2.6 m
MAXIMUM WEIGHT: 230 kg
CONSERVATION STATUS:
Insufficient information.

Description

Fraser's dolphin has a relatively robust body, with a large forehead extending almost to the tip of a short beak. The dorsal fin is triangular, very slightly hooked, and set at the body's mid-length. It has a complex colour pattern dominated by dark bluish-grey upper surfaces – the head, back, dorsal fin, flukes and flippers. The sides of the head and flanks are a paler grey, the belly white except the back quarter, which is dark. There are dark grey-blue stripes from the eyes and blowhole to the apex of the forehead. In adults, a broad dark stripe runs from the eye, along the flanks to the bottom of the back quarter of the body. A second dark stripe connects the base of the flipper and the mid-point of the lower jaw. Males and females of the species are of similar size and colour; both have 39 to 44 teeth on each jaw.

Where and when to view

This species occurs in the deep waters off southern Africa's east coast from about Port Elizabeth northwards, and is unlikely to be seen close inshore.

Biology

Fraser's dolphin was described only in 1956, and it wasn't until the early 1970s that a live specimen was identified as a new species. Even then, it was thought to be rare, and only in the 1980s was it established that at least several hundred thousand inhabited the world's oceans. As a result, very little is known about its biology and behaviour. Group sizes vary between four and 1 000 individuals. When in large schools, these animals can swim very fast – at 25 km/h and more – and they often 'porpoise' clear of the water when doing so. They apparently feed on both the fish and squid of the ocean's surface layers.

The sleek Fraser's dolphin is associated with the subtropical part of the Agulhas current off the eastern seaboard.

Spinner Dolphin

Stenella longirostris

TYPE: Toothed whale – dolphin
(Suborder Odontoceti,
Family Delphinidae)
MAXIMUM LENGTH: 2.4 m
MAXIMUM WEIGHT: 120 kg
CONSERVATION STATUS:
Insufficient information.

Description

This species is similar in form to the spotted dolphin, though the latter is slightly larger and less slender. The relatively large beak is long and narrow, the large, upright dorsal fin set at the body's mid-length. Beak, top of head, back, dorsal fin, flippers, flukes and the forward part of the flanks are a darkish grey. The posterior of the flanks and the underside of the body are lighter grey to white. There is a dark stripe from eye to flipper and from eye to apex of the forehead. Characteristic features are a dark, almost black, tip to the snout and the animal's habit of jumping clear of the water and 'spinning' on the longitudinal axis (hence the common name).

Like the spotted dolphins, there appear to be two distinct stocks of the species in the region's waters. Those at the southern end of the range – northern KwaZulu-Natal – appear to be larger than the more northerly, warmer-water animals (2.2 m compared to about 1.9 m).

Where and when to view

These are the most commonly seen dolphins in the western Indian ocean. Unfortunately, though, they seldom venture close to land. Nevertheless, they can occasionally be observed anywhere north of the Richard's Bay area.

Biology

Spinner dolphins occur in the tropical waters of both the Atlantic and Indian Oceans. In the southern African region, the Atlantic species, *Stenella clymene*, apparently occurs off northern Namibia and Angola and is not covered here.

Migratory movements are not known, though the species is found off northern KwaZulu-Natal and Mozambique throughout the year. Spinner dolphins gather in large groups, often of more than 100 individuals. In the Indian Ocean region, groups of several hundred, often mixed with spotted dolphins, occur regularly and will swim rapidly, 'porpoising' clear of the water, towards any passing vessel to ride the bow-wave. Spinner dolphins are fast swimmers, easily able to keep pace with a vessel travelling at around 30 km/h. Groups are also seen in bays, just outside fringing coral reefs or around islands – probably because these areas are rich in fish and squid, and provide relatively safe resting grounds. There have been reports of spinner dolphins entering the bay area of the Bazaruto Archipelago at spring tides to chase fish into the shallow waters.

Spinner dolphin calves, about 80 cm in length, are born after a gestation period of around one year. Like their spotted cousins, large numbers were killed in the Pacific tuna fishing operations, but that cause of mortality has been virtually eliminated. They are, though, captured incidentally throughout most of their range in the western Indian Ocean.

Distinctive features include a dark dorsal 'cape'.

Risso's Dolphin

Grampus griseus

TYPE: Toothed whale – dolphin
(Suborder Odontoceti, Family Delphinidae)
MAXIMUM LENGTH: 3 m
MAXIMUM WEIGHT: 320 kg
CONSERVATION STATUS:
Insufficient information.

Description

This dolphin superficially resembles the pilot whale but is a more slender animal, particularly behind the large, high dorsal fin. The head is bulbous but less so than in the pilot whale, and there is no beak. A shallow V-shaped vertical groove runs through the midline of the forehead. The flippers are long (up to one-fifth of the body length); the back and sides of the body are dark grey-blue, becoming paler towards the under surface. There is a light grey to white anchor-shaped patch across the chest between the flippers. Older dolphins carry numerous whitish scars and streaks, giving the animal – and especially its head – a whitish appearance. In our region, these dolphins are some 60 cm smaller than their northern hemisphere counterparts. The scars are probably caused by inter-species fights, and by the squid that the dolphin hunts.

Risso's dolphin, though widely distributed, occurs in deep waters and is seldom seen. Note the scarring on this specimen.

The dolphin is usually found in small groups. Some old specimens appear almost completely white from the scars they carry.

Where and when to view

Distributed throughout the region, but is unlikely to be seen close inshore. Strandings, however, frequently occur.

Biology

This dolphin inhabits southern African waters throughout the year and does not appear to migrate. It forms fairly small (up to 15-strong) groups, but schools of several thousand have been recorded. It is most often observed moving and surfacing slowly, or almost stationary in the water as though resting. Bow-riding and aerial behaviour have also been observed.

Risso's dolphin feeds predominantly on squid, some of which are fairly deep-water and light-emitting species – which suggests that the animals are capable of diving to fair depths, and that they may use sight, as well as echolocation, to find and catch their prey.

Dusky Dolphin

Lagenorhynchus obscurus

TYPE: Toothed whale – dolphin
(Suborder Odontoceti, Family Delphinidae)
MAXIMUM LENGTH: 2 m
MAXIMUM WEIGHT: 90 kg
CONSERVATION STATUS:
Insufficient information.

Description

This is a small dolphin, though its body is quite
chunky. The forehead slopes gently, almost to the tip of the
upper jaw, giving the species a characteristic short yet distinct
beak. The dorsal fin is relatively large for the animal's size, high
and pointed at the tip. The colour pattern is complex and very
distinctive. The jaws, back, dorsal fin, flukes and flippers are
black; the sides, in line with the forehead to about two thirds the
way along the body, are whitish and merge with the white belly,
extending over the front two thirds of the under
surface. There is also an irregularly shaped
whitish area on the sides, behind the dorsal fin
and on the dorsal fin itself. There are 28 to 32
teeth on each jaw.

Where and when to view

The dusky dolphin occurs in the cooler waters of
the southern hemisphere, with records from
New Zealand, Tasmania, Kerguelen, southern South America,
the Falkland Islands and the mid-South Atlantic Ocean. In our
region, it is found in the cold west coast waters as far north as
Angola, but does not extend farther east than False Bay on the
southern coast. It can be seen opportunistically in many bays
and inlets from False Bay (where large schools, of several hundred
individuals, have been observed) up the West Coast.

This is a very 'tourist
friendly' animal, readily riding
the bow-waves of passing
boats; performing the most
spectacular of aerial displays;
leaping several metres clear of
the water, sometimes in full
somersaults, and belly-flop-
ping back.

Biology

Very little is known of the
dusky dolphin in southern
African waters. Generally, it is
associated with the cold-water
Benguela current, which runs
northwards up the subcontinent's western seaboard from
the Cape of Good Hope to

*Dusky dolphins are renowned
for the way they ride the bow
waves of boats.*

The dusky dolphin is widely distributed within the southern hemisphere. In the southern Africa region, however, it occurs only in the cooler waters off the subcontinent's western seaboard.

northern Angola. In this area it occurs in shallow inshore waters, in bays, and in the deeper waters beyond the continental shelf's edge. In some areas it appears to occur only sporadically, possibly as a result of localized changes in water temperature and/or food supply.

The dusky dolphin's diet comprises fish and squid and, when feeding, it sometimes forms very large schools, though groups of 20 or so individuals are more common. In the region, it appears that the animal remains in deeper water at night and comes inshore during the day, possibly to rest and/or avoid predation. In other areas, dusky dolphins display a quite distinct pattern of seasonal movements, which seem to be related to the distribution and occurrence of their primary prey.

Other than chance records of whistles and clicks, not very much is known of the capacity of the dusky dolphin's echolocation system. Nor do we have a great deal of information on its reproductive cycle although, in New Zealand, birth and mating seem to occur principally in summer.

Humpback dolphin

Sousa chinensis

TYPE: Toothed whale – dolphin
MAXIMUM LENGTH: 2.7 m
MAXIMUM WEIGHT: 250 kg
CONSERVATION STATUS: Insufficiently known.
Although it is suspected that this species may be
Endangered, Vulnerable or Rare, there is not
enough information available to place it any of
these categories.

Description

Humpback dolphins normally occur in small groups of three to
seven individuals that move slowly and cryptically just behind
the surf line. Unlike bottlenose dolphins, they seldom surf or
jump. They reach a length of about 2.7 m, have a robust body,
a long and relatively narrow beak, and flippers that are rounded
at the tips. The dorsal fin is small and hooked, set on a broad,
distinctive 'hump' that is clearly visible as the animal breaks the
surface, as is the white-tipped jaw. The upper body is brownish
grey, the belly a little paler. Males are considerably bigger and
more robust than females.

Where and when to view

Humpback dolphins occur in the inshore region (rarely in water
more than 15 m deep) everywhere along the south and east
coasts of southern Africa – that is, to the east of False Bay.
Nowhere, however, are they plentiful. Their small group size
and cryptic behaviour render the animals inconspicuous, but the
patient watcher is often rewarded. They can be seen throughout
the year, almost anywhere off these coasts, though observation
is best at sites close to bays, river mouths and capes. Known vantage points include the Bazaruto Archipelago, the Sacco de
Inhaca and Inhaca Island (Maputo) in Mozambique; Richards
Bay, Nahoon Point (East London), Bird Rock (Port Elizabeth),
Lookout Beach (Jeffrey's Bay) and, especially, the Robberg
Peninsula at Plettenberg Bay.

Biology

Not much is known of the biology of humpback dolphins, mostly
because they are so few in number and difficult to observe.
Nevertheless, it appears very similar to that of the bottlenose
dolphins. After one year's gestation period
calves, weighing nearly 14 kg and about a metre
in length, are born throughout the year, though
most births occur in spring and summer. The
mother remains in close attendance until her
offspring can breathe and swim properly. The calf
takes its first solid food at about six months,
though suckling may continue for several years.
The interval between successive births is about
four years. Females reach sexual maturity at around ten years of
age, two to three years earlier than males. Lifespan, which is the
same for both sexes, may be more than 40 years.

Humpback dolphins are not great wanderers. In one
instance, several animals identified off Port Elizabeth were seen
in Cape St Francis Bay some weeks later. However, the nature
and exact extent of their movements, or migrations, is not

*The species is readily identified by the distinctive hump on its
back, situated beneath the dorsal fin.*

The humpback dolphin is a common sight off southern Africa's coasts throughout the year.

known, but they do not seem to range across too wide an area. Over several years of study, not one of 70 individuals identified and photographed off KwaZulu-Natal, has been re-sighted in Algoa Bay, some 1 400 km away. The composition of schools remains unknown; group members appear to join and leave at random, but over several months some stable affiliations have been observed, particularly between females. The species seems to feed only on the rising tide, its diet comprising the reef and estuarine-associated fish that are common in the close inshore waters of the region.

Humpback dolphins show heavy scarring from shark bites, and sharks are probably a major cause of death. The dolphins live close inshore, which makes them, like bottlenose dolphins, particularly vulnerable to man's activities. They accumulate high levels of pollutants, amounts which may well inhibit their capacity to reproduce effectively; they are regularly captured in nets – shark nets in KwaZulu-Natal, where catches are high enough to be of concern for their continued survival in KwaZulu-Natal's waters, and in fishermen's nets in Mozambique, where unknown numbers are caught each year. They are easily disturbed by boats and are sensitive to coastal development, so much so that Port Elizabeth has declared Algoa Bay's inshore area a 'go slow' zone. There is concern for the continued survival of the species throughout the Indo-Pacific region.

Common Dolphin

Delphinus delphis

TYPE: Toothed whale – dolphin
(Suborder Odontoceti, Family Delphinidae)
MAXIMUM LENGTH: 2.5 m
MAXIMUM WEIGHT: 175 kg
CONSERVATION STATUS:
Insufficient information.

Description

Common dolphins generally occur in groups of 200 or more and are often associated with diving birds, feeding whales and penguins. This is a slender species with a gently sloping forehead, a long, distinct beak and a slightly hooked triangular dorsal fin. The upper surface is brownish-black, the under surface creamy white. A characteristic elongated 'figure of eight', orange-brown towards the head and faint yellowish grey toward the back, can be seen on the flank. The dark colour of the back extends down into the 'criss cross' of the figure of eight, forming a 'saddle'. There are faint dark grey to black stripes from the corner of the mouth to the genital area, and another stripe from the lower jaw to the flipper. Common dolphins grow to a maximum of 2.5 m in length; adult males are slightly longer and heavier than the females.

The common dolphin occurs, often in huge schools, in all the temperate and tropical waters.

The aerial elegance of a common dolphin. The animal can swim at speeds of more than 35 km/h.

Where and when to view

As their name implies, these dolphins are widely distributed in all tropical and temperate waters. Although they have been recorded from the west coast of southern Africa, by far the majority of sightings and records are from the Western and Eastern Cape and KwaZulu-Natal. Along the Cape coasts, any high promontory should afford good viewing, especially in late summer and autumn when the animals aggregate in groups of several thousand. Here, the best spotting locality on the south coast is probably Plettenberg Bay, where huge schools can regularly be seen from the Robberg Peninsula. St Francis and Algoa bays and East London also offer potential but irregular sighting opportunities. During the 'sardine run' – a mass migration of fish, sharks, birds, dolphins and whales – the dolphins can be seen anywhere along the east coast as far north as Richards Bay.

Biology

Common dolphins occur in the southeast throughout the year but, in late summer and autumn, come together in huge schools in response to the seasonal appearance of small-fish and squid shoals. In autumn and early winter dolphin schools, averaging around 200 individuals, accompany the pilchards as they move slowly up the east coast in their annual 'sardine run'. The largest recorded aggregation covered 15 km² and contained more than 10 000 dolphins. Precisely why they so migrate is unknown, but obviously the richly nutritious pilchards provide a ready and substantial source of energy to females that have given birth to and are suckling calves.

Common dolphin schools are of mixed gender; the dominant males compete for and mate with as many females as possible. Generally, schools travel at about 7 km/h, though the dolphins can swim much more quickly, attaining speeds of over 35 km/h. When feeding, females and their calves appear to keep away from the other sex and size classes, probably to avoid competing for food resources.

The calving season is protracted over several months but peaks in summer. After a gestation period of around a year, a single 95-cm calf is born and is suckled for about six months, the mothers using the 'sardine run' to wean their calves. Females reach sexual maturity at about nine years of age, two years earlier than males. Both sexes may live for more than 40 years.

Common dolphins face the same threats as their bottlenose cousins: they are preyed upon by sharks; risk capture in fishing nets (especially gill nets) and accumulate high concentrations of industrial and agricultural pollutants, which mothers pass on to their young.

Bottlenose Dolphin

Tursiops truncatus

TYPE: Toothed whale – dolphin
(Suborder Odontoceti, Family Delphinidae)
MAXIMUM LENGTH: 2.5 to 3.3 m
MAXIMUM WEIGHT: 200 to 350 kg
CONSERVATION STATUS:
Insufficient information.

Description

Two similar forms of bottlenose dolphin, very much the same in appearance but differing in size, occur off southern Africa. The larger reaches over 3 m in length and occurs close inshore on the region's west coast. Along the south and east coasts it inhabits the deeper, oceanic waters and is not likely to be seen from the shore unless stranded.

The smaller form attains only 2.5 m in length, is found only off the east and south coasts (more or less east of Cape Agulhas), and lives in the shallow, inshore sea, seldom venturing into waters deeper than 30 m. Only the small, south and east coast form, which is far more likely to be seen, is described here.

The bottlenose dolphin's entire upper body, back, dorsal fin, flippers, flukes and head are dark grey in coloration. From about the midline, the sides of the body and head become paler, while the chest and belly are white. A number of dark stripes run from the eyes to its blowhole.

Bottlenose dolphins generally occur in groups of between ten and about 60 individuals, and are commonly observed close inshore, surfing and 'porpoising' in and out of breakers.

Although they can be, and often are, confused with common and humpback dolphins, the former seldom come into the surf zone while the latter are discernably less boisterous and occur only in small groups of up to ten individuals.

Where and when to view

The species is found in coastal areas throughout the south-eastern Cape. It surfs and feeds just behind the waves, and can best be observed from coastal cliffs and headlands.

Biology

Calves, nearly 14 kg in weight and a metre in length, are born throughout the year after a gestation period of about a year,

The basic social unit of the bottlenose dolphin is a group of related females.

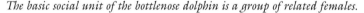

though most births occur between spring and summer. The mother closely attends her offspring and monitors its respiration as it swims high on her flank and in her slipstream. Its first few weeks are spent learning to swim and regulate its breathing, and it becomes progressively more independent. Between six months and a year it takes solid food, though suckling continues for three or four years, at which time the mother again mates. Females reach sexual maturity at about nine or ten years of age – two to three years earlier than males. Both sexes can live for more than 40 years.

Schools vary in composition according to activity but females and calves, all of whom are related, seem to form the basic unit. They are accompanied by one or more wandering mature males. Generally, these animals feed twice a day, in the early morning and evening. Mothers and calves come close inshore to take small sandy-bottom and reef-associated fish and squid. The rest feed farther out and on larger prey. Mothers and calves eat the same species and sizes of prey, which suggests that there is substantial parental guidance.

Contrary to common belief, sharks prey extensively on dolphins, chiefly the young, old and infirm. These animals also face other dangers, notably from the proliferation of gill nets in the inshore zones of countries looking for cheap and easy ways to feed their expanding human populations. Bottlenose dolphins also accumulate industrial (PCB) and agricultural (DDT) pollutants that are washed down rivers and taken up in the marine food chain. In some areas the pollution levels are high enough to affect the birth processes and to pose a threat

during infancy: suckling calves receive the mother's accumulated load through her milk. Although the precise effects of these massive toxin doses on the young have not been quantified, similar doses have killed baby monkeys. Such dolphins also suffer the effects of coastal development, and of poor farming practices that create erosion, the runoff damaging the inshore reefs.

These animals, which occur in groups of up to 60, are often seen close to the shore, weaving and 'porpoising' among the breakers.

Heaviside's Dolphin

Cephalorhynchus heavisidii

TYPE: Toothed whale – dolphin
(Suborder Odontoceti, Family Delphinidae)
MAXIMUM LENGTH: 1.8 m
MAXIMUM WEIGHT: 75 kg
CONSERVATION STATUS: Insufficient information; occurs only in southern African waters and population size is unknown.

Description

These are small dolphins – males and females are about the same size – and, like dusky dolphins, relatively 'chunky' in form with a conically shaped head, a long, gently sloping forehead and a short beak. The dorsal fin is shaped like an obtuse triangle and sits fairly low down on the back; the flippers are relatively large and rounded at the tips.

The colour pattern, though complex, is dominated by black, white and grey. Head, back, flukes, dorsal fin and flippers are black, contrasting with a white under surface, which extends backwards from about two-thirds of the body length in three white streaks, one at the midline and one on each side. Light

Heaviside's dolphin, distinguished by its triangular fin, is endemic to southern Africa.

grey areas can also be discerned on the sides of the the animal's body. There are 25 to 30 teeth in each jaw.

Where and when to view

Heaviside's dolphins occur only in southern Africa, their range apparently limited to the Benguela current system, between Cape Point and somewhere in Angola. As with most cetaceans, their movements and behaviour are unpredictable, and sightings are more a matter of luck than anything else. Nevertheless, they are said to be seen quite often off Lambert's Bay, on the West Coast of South Africa, and appear to be the most frequently sighted dolphins off Namibia, being especially common off Lüderitz. They attract numbers of tourists to both these centres. There are unsubstantiated reports of a school off Lambert's Bay that responds to human summonses, and which will travel with passing boats for hours on end. Because of their apparent rarity, every effort should be made to see them.

Biology

Despite its exclusivity to southern African waters, very little is known of this animal's behaviour or biology. Birthing and mating seem to be seasonal; calves are around 0.85 m long at birth.

Generally, Heaviside's dolphins are found close inshore, in waters of less than 20 m in depth, although there have been sightings of this species up to 100 km offshore. Mostly, the species occurs in small groups of up to 20 individuals, but may, at some times and in some areas, occur in groups of more than 150 dolphins. Unlike dusky dolphins, the animal is relatively cryptic in behaviour, seldom performing aerial displays.

Heaviside's dolphins consume both fish and squid. Recent research, involving the attachment of transmitters tuned to orbiting satellites, suggests that the species feeds at night or early in the morning; that it may range farther offshore than previously thought; and that some dolphins may remain in an area for a fair length of time (that is, they are semi-resident). Research on the animal is in its infancy, but some exciting information is already at hand.

Heaviside's dolphins are captured incidentally in fishing activity off the South African and Namibian (and possibly Angolan) coasts. The extent of the mortality, its effect on the population and its long-term influence on the survival of the species, however, are unknown. But if the death rate is anything like that of other members of the genus (Hector's dolphin in New Zealand, for instance), then our region's population may well be threatened.

Striped (Euphrosyne) Dolphin

Stenella coeruleoalba

TYPE: Toothed whale – dolphin
(Suborder Odontoceti, Family Delphinidae)
MAXIMUM LENGTH: 2.6 m
MAXIMUM WEIGHT: 160 kg
CONSERVATION STATUS: Insufficient information.

Description

The striped dolphin is a moderately robust animal with a fairly long beak and a slightly hooked dorsal fin that is set about mid length along the body. Coloration is quite complex: the upper surface from the beak back to just behind the dorsal fin is dark blue-grey; the flanks and the sides of the head above the eye are pale grey, though a swathe of dark blue-grey comes forward from just under the fin. The back quarter of the under surface is also dark blue-grey and there is a dark stripe from here to the eye, which separates the grey of the flanks from the white under surfaces. This stripe has a short branch above the base of the flipper. There is also a short, dark stripe from the eye to the flipper and from the eye to the corner of the mouth.

Where and when to view

The species is unlikely to be seen close inshore, though frequent strandings occur.

Biology

Little is known of the biology and behaviour of these animals, and what is known has been gleaned from the 140 or so individuals that have stranded on the southern African (mostly Eastern Cape) seaboard. The pattern and timing of the strandings suggests that the species' movements along the coast are subject to seasonal shift. Striped dolphins feed predominantly on deep-sea fish, notably lantern fish, squid and even some deep-sea shrimps – which indicates that the dolphin is a deep diver.

Striped dolphins normally occur in fairly large groups, some of them several hundred strong. They are fast swimmers, reaching speeds of up 28 km/h.

Southern Right Whale Dolphin

Lissodelphis peronii

TYPE: Toothed whale – dolphin
(Suborder Odontoceti, Family Delphinidae)
MAXIMUM LENGTH: 3 m
MAXIMUM WEIGHT: 130 kg
CONSERVATION STATUS:
Insufficient information.

Description

Like the right whale, the southern right whale dolphin does not have a dorsal fin – a similarity that confers the common name. This, and a distinctive colour pattern, renders the species quite unmistakable. The upper surface of the animal, from the top of its head to the flukes, is a blue-black, a colour that extends in a bow shape on the front half of the flanks down to the flippers. The upper surface of the flukes are light grey, while their underside is white.

Where and when to view

In our region, southern right whale dolphins have been recorded only off Lüderitz (Namibia), though they may occur elsewhere along the subcontinent's western seaboard. This is, nevertheless, a deep-water species and unlikely to be seen close inshore.

Biology

Southern right whale dolphins are rarely seen at sea and there are no recorded strandings in the region. Consequently, nothing is known of their biology, in the region, and behaviour is known only from a few at-sea sightings. The species appears to form schools of between several tens and more than 1 000 individuals. These animals are energetic swimmers, often 'porpoising' clear of the water in low-angle leaps when travelling at speed. In other regions, they feed on deep-sea fish and squid. They are often observed in association with other dolphins.

This dolphin is a deep-water animal, and rarely seen in the region.

Dugong

Dugong dugon

TYPE: Dugong
(Order Sirenia, Family Dugongidae)
MAXIMUM LENGTH: 3.0 m
MAXIMUM WEIGHT: 500 kg
CONSERVATION STATUS:
Vulnerable (possibly Endangered).

Description

The dugong has a large, rotund body, no discernible neck and a relatively small head and small eyes. The muzzle is large, fleshy, blunt and bristly. A fleshy, prehensile upper lip overhangs the mouth and terminates in a horseshoe-shaped disc. The males have short tusks, which are present but not erupted in the females. The flippers are broad and slightly pointed at the tip and the tail, much like that of a whale, is crescent shaped (and unlike manatees, which have spatulate shaped tails). There is a distinct ridge along the hind half of the back. The overall colour is a uniform light grey to tawny brown.

Where and when to view

Though vagrant dugongs have been recorded as far south as central Umhlali, KwaZulu-Natal, their normal range is from Maputo Bay northwards. However, their numbers in that bay have declined dramatically in recent years. The best places for dugong viewing are Linga Linga Point, Inhambane Bay and within the Bazaruto Archipelago.

Biology

Dugongs occur in tropical waters throughout the western Indian Ocean and also along the Indian, Asian and northern Australian coasts. They were once regarded as the only truly herbivorous marine mammal, consuming only sea-grasses (true flowering plants, not algae), though recent evidence indicates that they also eat small sea animals. They may consume up to 25 per cent of their body weight in sea-grass each day.

Although dugongs have an estimated lifespan of some 70 years, they reproduce slowly. Females become sexually mature at about 10 years of age, the gestation is 12 months, and females bear a single calf, up to 1.2 m in length, at intervals of three to seven years. Calves are suckled for up to 18 months.

Family bonds appear to be strong; there are eye-witness accounts of males attempting to free females or juveniles caught in nets.

Dugongs are gregarious, usually found in large herds which, historically, sometimes numbered more than 600 animals, though groups of less than 20 are now more common. They swim slowly, just beneath the surface, and in the clear waters off Mozambique they can clearly be seen from the air against the light-coloured sands. Like dolphins, they swim with an up-and-down movement of the tail. Dugongs are quiet animals, making practically no sound and creating little disturbance even when surfacing to breathe, which they do every three minutes or so. They will make off if approached by a motorboat, but are less wary of anchored craft (though they leave if the occupants make a noise).

The dugong is a coastal species, inhabiting the warm, shallow waters that sustain an abundance of the sea-grasses. This makes them particularly vulnerable to coastal-zone development and over-exploitation – their decline is directly related to the increasing human presence. Hunting, the nets of fishermen, coastal development and environmental degradation have all taken their toll.

The slow-moving dugong: seen mainly off Mozambique.

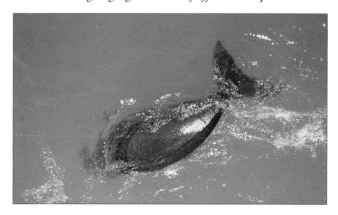

Cape Fur Seal

Arctocephalus pusillus

TYPE: Eared seal, fur seal (Family Otariidae)
MAXIMUM LENGTH: 2.7 m
MAXIMUM WEIGHT: 350 kg (males)
CONSERVATION STATUS: Plentiful, especially on South Africa's southern and west coasts and the Namibian coast. They are not in any danger of depletion.

Description

This is the largest of the southern hemisphere's fur seals. Adult males are bigger than the females, which are generally less than 2 m in length and weigh under 100 kg. The head and face are very dog-like, with a prominent snout and up to 30 coarse, protruding whiskers. The ears are short, tubular, hairless and pointed at the tips. Adult males are brownish-grey and develop a thick mane of rough fur on the neck and shoulders; females are olive brown to brown, with a tawny stripe at the jawline. Pups are black when born, becoming olive grey when they moult at about a year old. At sea, sleeping seals lie on their sides, with their heads down and a flipper raised.

Where and when to view

Single seals can be seen anywhere along the southeastern and western Cape coasts, often coming ashore to rest or if they are injured. Other than feeding aggregations at sea, large concentrations can only be seen at rookeries (or colonies). These are quite widely distributed in the southern African region from Algoa Bay in the east through to Cape Frio, on the Namibian coast, in the west.

Most of the rookeries are on offshore islands and access is difficult. However, there is a newly developing and easily observed colony on Plettenberg Bay's Robberg Peninsula (Cape south coast). The huge concentration at Cape Cross, north of Swakopmund in Namibia, is fairly accessible, though an entry permit is required (see also page 17).

Biology

Cape fur seals do not migrate but, rather, range far and wide in quest of food. However, they may spend up to half the year at their rookeries. At sea they hunt singly, gathering together at shoals of fish or squid. When food is plentiful (in captivity, for instance), they eat from 6 to 8 per cent of their body weight each day. They are quick through the water, capable of speeds of up to 16 km/h; and agile, often leaping clear of the water (or 'porpoising').

This is the only seal indigenous to southern Africa; the largest concentration is to be found north of Namibia's Swakopmund.

Mother and child. Bulls lord it over harems comprising about 20 females.

Adult breeding bulls come ashore to set up territories on the rookeries in late October. The cows follow soon after, moving into the males' territories, or harems. The bull's harem contains about 20 cows, and he will defend it against all comers. The pups, which are born in late November and early December, are about 75 cm long at birth and are suckled for almost a year, although they begin to take solid food from about six months. Bulls mate with their females about six days after the birth. Rookeries are noisy places, the adult bulls roaring over disputed territory, and individuals of both sexes grunting during the frequent fights and when they are at play. Cows also utter howls, and pups bleat like lambs. The rookeries are also good places to see one of the seal's major predator's – the great white shark.

The region's fur seal numbers have increased dramatically in recent years while, at the same time, many of the major fish stocks have declined. Blame has, naturally, been attached to the seals and there have been calls for a culling programme. Unhappily the facts support the accusations: Cape fur seals, especially young males, are notorious scavengers, often stealing fish or squid from fishermen's lines. As a result, many are shot at sea. They also steal from trawlers and many becoming entangled in the nets – where they either drown or are killed when hauled aboard. All of which represents a serious dilemma for the fisheries scientist and the conservationist, who must somehow reconcile the well-being of the seals with the very valid interests, indeed with the livelihood, of the fishermen.

Seals of the Far South

A number of seal species occasionally visit the southern African region as vagrants from their breeding grounds in the southern latitudes. Rarely seen and then mostly in summer, they include the crabeater, leopard and southern elephant seals (though these appear on our coasts quite regularly), all three of which belong to the Family Phocidae – the 'earless' or true seals. They are distinguished from 'eared' seals by the absence of an external ear and by their form of locomotion: they are unable to turn their hind limbs forwards, and cover the ground with a caterpillar-like shuffling motion of the body. Nor can their forelimbs give much support. In the water, these seals swim with a sinuous side-to-side movement of body and hind limbs.

Crabeater Seal

Lobodon carcinophagus

TYPE: True seal (Family Phocidae)
MAXIMUM LENGTH: 2.6 m
MAXIMUM WEIGHT: 230 kg
CONSERVATION STATUS: Plentiful; the global population is at least 7 million, and faces no human threat.

A slender marine mammal with a small head and relatively long, rounded snout. It occurs throughout the Antarctic pack-ice areas; southern African records are all from the Western and Eastern Cape coasts. Just after the moult, the adult's upper body is dark grey, the underparts paler. This coloration gradually fades.

OPPOSITE: Antarctic fur seal. ABOVE: Southern elephant seal.

Southern Elephant Seal

Mirounga leonina

TYPE: True seal (Family Phocidae)
MAXIMUM LENGTH: 4.2 m
MAXIMUM WEIGHT: 3 t
CONSERVATION STATUS: The world population, estimated at around 650 000, is in decline.

The adult male of this species, which is widely distributed in sub-Antarctic waters, is the largest of all seals; females are much smaller. The bull's most characteristic feature is its fleshy snout (or proboscis), an extension of the nostrils which develops as the animal matures. Although these massive seals are only vagrants to our coasts, they appear on beaches – as far north as Mozambique – quite regularly during the summer months.

Leopard Seal

Hydrurga leptonyx

TYPE: True seal (Family Phocidae)
MAXIMUM LENGTH: 3.4 m
MAXIMUM WEIGHT: 600 kg
CONSERVATION STATUS: There is no apparent human threat to the species; world population is at least 300 000.

The leopard seal, found throughout the Antarctic region (mostly near the pack-ice), is slender-bodied but has a robust, almost reptilian look to the head, jaws and neck. The adult's grey coloration is overlaid with numerous dark and light spots.

Antarctic Fur Seal

Arctocephalus gazella

TYPE: Eared seal (Family Otariidae)
MAXIMUM LENGTH: 2.1 m
MAXIMUM WEIGHT: 210 kg
CONSERVATION STATUS: Recovering from past exploitation; total world population is at least 1.3 million and increasing.

This animal, which lives in colonies on Marion, Prince Edward and other sub-Antarctic islands, looks very much like the Cape and sub-Antarctic fur seals, but is smaller than the former and slightly larger than the latter. Males are markedly larger than females; adults are silver-grey to brownish on the back and sides, gingery on the belly.

Sub-Antarctic Fur Seal

Arctocephalus tropicalis

TYPE: Eared seal (Family Otariidae)
MAXIMUM LENGTH: 1.8 m
MAXIMUM WEIGHT: 165 kg
CONSERVATION STATUS: Recovering from past exploitation; total world population is at least 310 000.

Much smaller than the Cape fur seal, this species lives in colonies on Tristan da Cunha, and on Gough, Marion and other sub-Antarctic islands. Males are bigger than females, and brownish-grey with a creamy or yellow chest, throat and face and a distinct cream-coloured crest of hairs on the forehead. Adult females are greyish above, brownish on the underparts, with a yellowish chest, throat and face.

The once endangered sub-Antarctic fur seal.

Useful Contacts

 **The MTN Whale Route,**
P.O. Box 797, Howard Place 7450;
tel: (021) 401 7347; fax: (021) 401 7303;
cellphone: 083 212 1075;

West Coast Publicity Association, P.O. Box 139,
Saldanha 7395; tel: (02281) 4 2088/58.

National Parks Board, P.O. Box 787,
Pretoria 0001; tel: (012) 343 1991; Cape Town:
P.O. Box 7400, Roggebaai 8012;
tel:(021) 22 2810.

 MTN Centre for Dolphin Studies,
P.O. Box 1856, Plettenberg Bay 6600;
cellphone: 082 677 4742;
e-mail: cdsvgc@iafrica.com

Cape Central Tourism Gateway, Lower Adderley Street;
P.O. Box 1403, Cape Town 8000; tel: (021) 418 5214/5;
e-mail: captour@iafrica.com

Cape Overberg Tourism Association, P.O. Box 250,
Caledon 7230; tel: (0281) 4 1466; e-mail: cota@capeover-
berg.co.za; Internet: www:http://capeoverberg.co.za

Garden Route Regional Tourism Office,
P.O. Box 1514, George 6530; tel: (044) 874 4040;
e-mail:gardenroute@pixie.co.za

Index

Credits

Picture credits read from top to bottom, starting with that at the top left of the page. Page numbers in bold indicate major species profiles. Abbreviations: PAPL=Photo Access Photographic Library; SIL= Struik Image Library

PHOTOGRAPHS
Shaen Adey/SIL: 22a, 23a, 23b, 24b, 26, 28a, 28b, 31a, 31b, 33b, 34a, 34b, 35a, 37a, 47b, back cover b; Robert Baldwin: 95; Roger de la Harpe/SIL: 33a; Nigel Dennis/SIL: 47a; Gerhard Dreyer: 22b; Gerhard Dreyer/SIL: 19a, 20b, 39a, 39c, 40b, 41a, 41b, 42a, 42b, 43a; Jean du Plessis: 18a, 18b, 18c, 18 d; Bruce Dyer: 92; Ken Findlay: front cover, 7, 20a, 32, 35b, 39b, 53, 59, 60, 89, back cover c & d; Rod Haestier: front cover, 5, 12, 16, 37b, 45b, 45c, 48/49, 50a, 50b, 51, 58, 90; John Haig: 8b, 11; Lex Hes: 100; Thierry Homas/BIOS: 98; Thomas Jefferson: 82, 83, 88; Leszek Karczmarski: 86; Walter Knirr/SIL: 19b, 46; Sasa Kralj/iAfrica: 24a; Pierre Malan: 94; Mike Meyer: 70; Colin Mostert: 84; Doug Perrine/PAPL: 91; Sea Fisheries

Research Institute: 10a, 10b, 10c; Mark Skinner: 29b; Philip van den Berg: 97; Philip van den Berg/HPH: 40a, 96, back cover a; Michel Vely: 74; John Visser: 99; Hein von Hörsten/SIL: 19c, 30, 38, 45a; Lanz von Hörsten/SIL: 29a; P. Wagner/PAPL: 47c; James D. Watt/PAPL: 78, 79; Christian Weis/BIOS: 76.

ILLUSTRATIONS
David Thorpe: 52, 55, 56/7, 61, 62, 63, 64, 65, 66, 68, 71, 72, 73, 77, 80, 81, 85, 87. The illustration on page 8 is from an original (1897) painting by F. Linder; published courtesy the South African Maritime Museum, Cape Town; photograph by John Haig. That on page 9 is a reproduction of a work by Sir William Jardine, dated 1836 and published as Plate 4 of Volume 12 (Whales) of the Naturalist's Library; published courtesy of The British Museum of Natural History, London. The illustrations on pages 6, 13, 14 and 15 are published by courtesy The MTN Whale Route.